TALES OF INDIAN CHIVALRY

TALES OF INDIAN CHIVALRY

MICHAEL MACMILLAN

GYAN

Published by

GYAN

Gyan Publishing House
5, Ansari Road
Daryaganj, New Delhi-110002
Phone: 011-47034999, 9811692060
E-mail: books@gyanbooks.com

Distribution Network
gyanbooks.com
India, USA, Canada, UK, Australia

ISBN: 978-93-7097-091-5 (PB)

First Published, 1901

2nd Impression 2025

Printed at: Gyan Press, Delhi.

TALES OF INDIAN CHIVALRY
Arthur MICHAEL MACMILLAN

Tales of Indian Chivalry

M 748

"MET IN FULL CAREER IN THE CENTRE OF THE ARENA"

Tales of Indian Chivalry

BY

MICHAEL MACMILLAN

Principal of Elphinstone College, Bombay

Illustrated by Paul Hardy

BLACKIE AND SON LIMITED
WARWICK HOUSE, BOMBAY
LONDON AND GLASGOW

CONTENTS

ILLUSTRATIONS

TALES
OF
INDIAN CHIVALRY

SAVED FROM THE FLAMES

I

MORE than three hundred years ago a gallant band of Mogul troopers, two hundred strong, was passing along the borders of Rajputana on their way to join the army of the great Akbar, who was then engaged in the conquest of Gujarat. Their burnished armour flashed, and their gay scarves of various colours shone bravely, in the rays of the setting sun. They were armed with two-handed broadswords, and shields and coats of mail. The whole force was splendidly equipped, and one might conjecture from the spick-and-span appearance of their arms and accoutrements that the troopers had not yet marched far from home. This was indeed the case. Abbas Khan, their leader, was the son and heir of a Mogul chieftain, whose castle they had left that very afternoon on their way to what was to many of them their first experience of war. He was a tall and handsome young man, and his face glowed with youthful enthusiasm as he anticipated the martial honours that he hoped to win under the standard of his heroic emperor.

At a distance of a few miles another gay cavalcade, but of a different character, was converging upon the route of Abbas Khan's force. This other cavalcade was a peaceful one, composed of Hindus conducting a young bride to the home of the father of her boy husband, where she was to spend the rest of her life immured in the zenana[1]. She was carried in a closely-veiled litter, which not only shielded her from the eyes of passers-by, but also prevented her from breathing the fresh air of heaven and enjoying the beautiful scenery through which she was being carried to her new home among strangers. Soon after sunset, as they were passing along the banks of the river Rohini at the place where

[1] Zenana = the part of a house in which women are secluded.

the Hindus burnt their dead, their peaceful progress was suddenly interrupted. A band of robbers pounced upon them, and with little trouble overpowered the few Rajputs who formed the bride's escort. They then seized the litter, and, tearing it open with rude hands, drew the fair occupant into the open air.

Tulsibai stared with wild alarm on the fierce figures by which she was surrounded. Poor girl, she was only fifteen years old, and in her home, as the only child and idol of her parents, had been brought up in the lap of luxury, and carefully shielded from the slightest cause of annoyance. It was too terrible for her to be thus suddenly exposed to the tender mercies of bandits, whom in her childish ignorance she mistook for the demons of her fairy-tales. If beauty could charm the savage beast, she had enough of that to move them to pity. But they were utterly insensible to the pleading gaze of her dark eyes, and sternly ordered her to hand over the jewels in which she was richly decked. From sheer terror she was unable to obey. Her trembling fingers refused to detach the pearls from her ears, nose, and neck, and the gold bangles from her ankles and wrists.

Rough hands would soon have stripped her not only of jewels, but also of her rich embroidered garments, had it not been for the sudden appearance upon the scene of Abbas Khan and his following. The robbers, unable to resist such a force, fled precipitately, pursued by some twenty of the Mogul troopers. Tulsibai remained seated on the ground, a picture of misery, scarcely realizing that she had escaped from the perils by which she had been surrounded. Her countenance, however, soon began to brighten when her young deliverer approached. If the robbers were *rakshasas*[1], he was surely a god. Never had she seen in human form anything so grand and beautiful as this handsome young soldier in all the glory of his martial panoply. Nor had he ever seen anything so lovely as Tulsibai, as she sat there before him with her lustrous eyes full of tears, and with her loveliness cunningly set off by her bridal array.

For him, at any rate, it was a case of love at first sight. As with tender care he helped her into her litter, wild thoughts came surging

[1] Rakshasas = demons.

through his brain. He would carry her off to his father's castle, or to some refuge in the jungle, where, forgotten by the world, they could live a life of joy and love. Then flashed through his mind his duty to the noble emperor whom he served, his honour as a soldier, and the baseness of taking advantage of the helplessness of a weak girl. After a sharp mental struggle, honour won the day, and before Tulsibai's attendants came back from their hiding-places, he had resolved to follow the path of duty, however sore his heart might be.

Abbas Khan escorted Tulsibai's party until they were in sight of her father-in-law's mansion. He rode beside her litter absorbed in deep thought. He could not see her, but she could, and did, take peeps at him through the curtains, and every look roused in her heart strange feelings of affection and admiration for the handsome stranger. At last they reach the point where their paths diverge, and must separate for ever. Abbas Khan bids her farewell in a voice which he vainly tries to steady. She, regardless of convention, draws aside the curtain of the litter and drops into the hand of her deliverer a diamond ring. Their eyes meet for the last time in a long gaze of love and despair, and they drift apart on the waves of life, he to war and glory, she to the new home her parents have chosen for her. No doubt she will be rebuked and endure heavy penance for her indiscretion, but neither rebuke nor penance will ever obliterate the image of her young deliverer from her heart. She may be married and be a good wife and mother in her Hindu home, but the dearest memory of her soul will be the thought of the godlike young stranger. And he, too, will never forget. Tulsibai is his first love, and in peace and in war, whatever his fortunes may be, he will often think with tender regret of the fair Hindu girl whom he saved from the robbers.

II

A year had passed away, and Abbas Khan once more rode by the banks of the Rohini. He was mounted on a splendid Arab horse that he had chosen as his share of the spoil after a great victory. His shield and helmet shone as brightly as before, but they were dinted with many a stroke of sword and javelin, for in the year that had passed, the young warrior had enjoyed his fill of hard fighting. He had stood beside Akbar in the fierce combat with the Mirzas among the cactus hedges near Surat, and had proved his manhood on many another hard-fought field. The war was now over, and Abbas Khan was returning to take possession of his ancestral domain, his father having died during his absence. It may be imagined that his heart was full of sadness, as he thought of the lonely home to which he was returning, and of the fair face he had seen for a moment and lost for ever in this very place. What to him were all the honour and glory he had won if he was to live alone in the world with only memories of those whom he loved? No doubt, in the course of time, youth and health would dissipate or mitigate his sorrows, but now, as he rode alone by the banks of the Rohini, melancholy reigned supreme in his soul, and even his noble steed seemed infected by his dejection.

With listless eyes he watched a long Hindu funeral procession that was winding its way to the burning ghat[1]. A large company of friends and relations were accompanying the

[1] Burning ghat=the place where the Hindus burn their dead.

bier of a boy, who, from the costly scarf in which his corpse was wrapped, and the number of the mourners, must have belonged to a rich and powerful family. The litter containing the dead body was borne by four bareheaded bearers, clad in silk. A long train of barelegged and barefooted men in turbans of funereal white walked before the bier, calling aloud on their god Rama in a monotonous and lugubrious chant, and at intervals scattering handfuls of rice and jowari[1] and small pieces of copper money by the wayside. The mourner who walked immediately before the feet of the corpse carried in an earthen vessel the fire from which the funeral pyre was to be lighted. There were two horses in the company. One bore a silent drum, and on the other rode a horseman with a furled flag.

Presently, when the procession reached the burning ghat, it became clear that the performance of the rite of *sati*[2] was contemplated. A woman was standing near the corpse, who was evidently the wife of the

[1] Jowari, a coarse species of millet.

[2] Sati = burning of a living widow on the funeral pyre of her dead husband.

(M 748)

dead boy, and was waiting to be consumed with him on the funeral pyre. The Emperor Akbar was strongly opposed to this cruel rite, and did all he could to suppress it, by enacting that no wife was to be so sacrificed except of her own free-will. Abbas Khan, who with the enthusiam of youth entered heart and soul into all the great ideas of the great emperor, immediately determined to see with his own eyes that the imperial edict was not violated in this particular case. So he cantered up to the funeral pyre, regardless of the scowls with which he was greeted by the Brahmins and mourners.

How describe his feelings when he discovered that the lady about to immolate herself was she whom he had met and saved on the banks of the Rohini twelve long months ago! Tulsi-bai's husband had been a sickly boy of ten or eleven years. She had been kind to him, so that he loved her as he loved none of his sisters, and would take his medicine from no other hands but hers. At last the fever from which he was suffering overpowered him, and he died.

The young widow had little to tempt her to live. The rules of caste prevented her from marrying again, even if she had wished to do so. Her beautiful hair would no longer be braided and anointed with fragrant oil and adorned with flowers. Instead of jewels and embroidered robes, she would be compelled to wear nothing but plain white. Worst of all, her husband's death would be regarded as the consequence of some unknown sins that she had committed, and she would be an evil omen and an object of loathing and contempt in the eyes of all who looked upon her. What wonder, then, that she lent a willing ear to the Brahmins when they told her how glorious a thing it would be for her to refuse to survive her husband? The quick agony of death on the funeral pyre seemed preferable to the protracted pain of an unhappy life. So she allowed herself to be led to the sacrifice, and was ready to face with the calm courage of despair the terrible death by which a Hindu wife shows the strength of her affection for her husband. There she stood, decked out for the last time in her jewels, the gold of which the greedy priests were eager to rake out from among the ashes of the dead. As Abbas Khan looked upon her, she seemed motionless and impassive as a marble statue.

But when she saw him whom she had never hoped to see again, the life blood flowed once more tumultuously through her veins and flushed her face. Hope began to revive in her breast, and she felt that it was sad to die so young and see no more the pleasant light of the sun.

Abbas Khan was moved even more by pity for her misfortunes than by admiration for her loveliness, although in the year that had elapsed since their last meeting she had developed from a graceful and pretty girl into a beautiful woman. He grasped the situation in a moment, and, riding up to the chief of the Brahmins, reminded him that the imperial edict forbade *sati*, unless the victim were herself willing to suffer. "Ask her yourself," replied the Brahmin; "she has herself of her own accord consented to die like a true and loving wife on her husband's funeral pyre." Abbas Khan then turned to the young widow and said: "Know that the great emperor allows no widow to be sacrificed against her will. Tell me, then, whether it is of your own freewill that you thus untimely hurl yourself into the other world." At these words the desire of life grew strong in the heart of the unhappy girl, and, stretching out her arms to the young soldier, she cried out, "My lord, you saved me once before. Ah, save me now, if you can, from these cruel men! But no, they are hungry for my death, and will slay you before me, if you withstand them. Quick, quick, away from this horrible place and leave me to my fate!"

On hearing Tulsibai's appeal for help the Brahmins, fearful of being baulked of their prey, declared that she had voluntarily come to her death, and that wild words uttered at the point of death could not be taken into account. At the same time they armed themselves with heavy sticks from the funeral pyre, and showed plainly that if the stranger chose to interfere they would use force. Upon this, Abbas Khan edged his horse nearer and nearer to Tulsibai, and eagerly whispered to her, "If I dismount, we are both lost. Place, then, your foot in my stirrup, grasp my right hand behind my back, and I will swing you up behind me. Once there, you may defy these ghouls[1]." The brave Rajput girl suited her action to his words, and, helped by her lover's strong right arm, leapt on to the

[1] Ghouls = monsters that eat dead bodies.

M 745

"THEN HE CHARGED THE ENEMY"

crupper. Abbas Khan immediately turned his horse's head homewards, and without much difficulty forced a way through the angry crowd.

When they had thus escaped from the burning ground, a new danger awaited them. Two Rajput soldiers, who happened to be riding in the neighbourhood, saw what was going on, but were too far away to prevent Abbas Khan from mounting Tulsibai on his horse behind him. They were unfortunately on the road that led to Abbas Khan's castle, and determined to bar the progress of the fugitives. There was no time to delay. Abbas Khan told his fair burden to take her hand from his sword-arm and hold firmly on to his belt instead. Then he charged the enemy, directing his force especially upon the Rajput on his right hand, who seemed the more powerful of the two. As they came to close quarters, one sword-cut fell on his shield, another on his helmet, but failed to check his course. He delivered a stunning blow with his sword, as he passed, on the head of the enemy on his left, and at the same time charged straight at the Rajput on the right, whose horse went down before the heavier steed of the Moslem and threw its rider in the dust. The other Rajput, dizzy with the blow he had received, shrank from continuing the combat single-handed against such a formidable antagonist, and preferred to dismount and assist his fallen comrade, leaving the path open to Abbas Khan. A short ride brought him to his father's castle, where he was soon after married to his Rajput bride.

Tulsibai's father was easily induced to acquiesce in what he could not prevent. He was very fond of his only daughter, and in his heart rejoiced that she had escaped the Indian widow's evil choice between a miserable life and death on her husband's funeral pyre. Abbas Khan had already won the Emperor Akbar's approval by his gallantry on the field of battle, and certainly did not lose ground in his favour by preventing a *sati* and marrying a Rajput wife. By both these actions he followed the lead of his emperor and identified himself with Akbar's imperial policy, as few of the Mogul aristocracy had been willing to do. The natural result was that he received many substantial marks of the emperor's favour, and became in course of time one of his greatest generals and most trusty councillors.

The Bride of the Padishah

I. THE WOOING

AHMED SHAH, the proud Padishah[1] of Sind, was holding high festival in his cool palace by the Silver Lake, to which he retreated from his capital in the hot months of summer. He was a strong, handsome, black-bearded man, in the prime of life, famous for his exploits in war and for his patronage of poetry, architecture, and other arts of peace. As with some chosen comrades he sailed by moonlight in his gilded pinnace among the wooded islands of the beautiful lake and listened to the songs and music of the bards who accompanied him, he seemed to be exalted to the highest pitch of human happiness. The Mahometan musicians in the boat with him sang of the Padishah's victories in war, of the Houris of Paradise, and of the loves of the rose and the bulbul. Then an

[1] Padishah = king.

Indian bard lifted up his voice in honour of a Rajput maiden, graceful as a gazelle, and wise and beautiful and modest as Sita, the wife of Rama. The magic strains of his poetry, heard beneath the bewitching rays of an Indian moon, made the Padishah fall in love with the beauty of the maiden so highly extolled in golden verses. "When did she live, this pearl among women," he asked, "and what accursed unbeliever was her spouse?" "She lives now and is still unwedded," replied the bard. "I celebrate the beauty of Lala, the only daughter of the Rajput chieftain, Purbut Singh." "If she is as lovely as you paint her, she must be my bride; if not, your head shall pay for your lying eulogy." Having so said, the king fell into deep thought and ordered his pinnace back to the marble landing-stage of the palace.

On the morrow Ahmed Shah sent for his principal Brahmin adviser and asked for information about Purbut Singh's daughter. The Brahmin in reply gave in serious prose an account of her beauty and accomplishments that entirely confirmed the poetic panegyric sung by the Hindu bard on the moonlit waters of the Silver Lake. This was enough for the amorous heart of the Padishah. Without further delay he told the Brahmin to signify to Purbut Singh that it was his will and pleasure to make Lala his bride. However, the course of his love was not destined to run quite smoothly. Several Rajputs had allowed their daughters to enter the harems of Ahmed Shah and his chief nobles, but Purbut Singh was a Rajput of Rajputs, who prided himself, above all things, on his stainless pedigree. He scorned the thought that a daughter of his should lose caste by marrying a Mahometan, even though by so doing she should share the throne of a powerful monarch. Nevertheless, to gain time he feigned compliance with the will of his suzerain. In the meantime he retired to his hill fortress Ahore, and called all his relations and vassals to defend him and his daughter against the contemplated insult.

Ahmed Shah, getting wind of these preparations, mustered a splendidly-appointed army of 10,000 men, which might, according to circumstances, either storm the Rajput castle or form an escort for his Rajput bride. He himself led the army, seated in a silver howdah on his state elephant, and accompanied by another elephant gorgeously caparisoned and prepared for the reception of the beautiful Lala.

In this manner Ahmed Shah rode boldly with his army close up to the walls of Ahore and demanded admission. The answer to the demand was an arrow shot with unerring skill, which stuck quivering on the crown above Ahmed Shah's howdah. On the arrow was a scroll containing the following message: "The archer who shot this arrow into the crown above thy head could as easily have shot it into the brain of the monkey-faced barbarian who presumes to woo the daughter of Purbut Singh. Be warned in time, and retire before a worse thing befalls thee." At the same time the rich dress that had been sent by the Padishah as *wusunt*[1] to his bride, according to the practice of Rajput marriage, was tossed contemptuously like a bundle of dirty clothes over the wall, and fell in the dust before the feet of Ahmed Shah's elephant. Thus war to the knife was declared. The Mahometan army, fearing that injury might be added to insult, retired from its exposed position with more precipitancy than dignity, lest a sudden

[1] Wusunt = bridal present.

discharge of Rajput arrows should follow the declaration of war.

Ahmed Shah's courting now took the form of a vigorously-prosecuted siege. Ahore was garrisoned by 3000 valiant Rajputs. The rich gifts of treasure, sent by Ahmed Shah to conciliate his bride and her father, had been spent on strengthening the defences of the walls and providing the garrison with the best weapons that money could purchase. When the besiegers approached the walls, they were shot down by arrows or overwhelmed with huge stones that had been collected on the tops of the ramparts. Sometimes the garrison allowed scaling-ladders to be erected against the walls, but pushed them back again with long poles before any of the enemy could reach the top, and so destroyed those of the besiegers who were struggling up the rungs. Every attempt to storm the fort was foiled, until the besiegers, finding the place impregnable, gave up assaulting the walls and had recourse to a rigorous investment.

The capture of the fortress now became merely a question of time. After two or three months the supply of provisions began to run short, and there was no hope of relief from outside. Purbut Singh might, no doubt, have obtained favourable terms of capitulation if he had consented to his daughter's marriage with the Padishah. This, however, he entirely refused to allow, and, without submission on this vital point, no terms of capitulation could be granted to the hard-pressed garrison.

The Rajputs determined to die rather than yield. But if they were killed, their wives and daughters would become the wives or concubines of the Mahometan conquerors. This pollution could only be averted by the terrible rite of *johur*, which consisted in first immolating all the women and children, and then rushing to death in a desperate attack upon the overwhelming forces of the enemy.

The women professed their readiness to play their part in the great tragedy. If some of them in their hearts were inclined to prefer dishonour to death, they did not venture to express their base sentiments, which would have merely exposed them to opprobrium without saving their lives. Some few obtained permission to put on martial harness and join their husbands, fathers, and brothers in the coming battle. The wife of Purbut Singh, with no trace of fear or regret on her countenance, told her husband that she and the other women would destroy themselves on the funeral pyre and meet those near and dear to them in heaven rather than become the slaves of the Moslem. A huge funeral pyre was raised at night. Into this were first flung all the jewels and other valuables that were in the fortress. Then the women, old and young, leapt with their children into the flames or fell upon the sword, until not a single Rajputni[1], old or young, was left alive.

In the morning it was the turn of the men to immolate themselves and find an easier death by the sword of the enemy. The great act of devotion had to be performed with all due ceremony. They put sprigs of the sacred *toolsi*[2] in their helmets, and tied the stone called *saligram* round their necks, and on their heads the coronet that symbolized their nuptials with the divine *Apsaras*, the fair ones of heaven. Then, 2500 strong, they assembled at daybreak, clad in saffron robes, inside the great gate of the fortress, and embraced one another tenderly as men who would never meet again. The gate was

[1] Rajputni = Rajput woman. [2] Toolsi = basil.

thrown open, and, headed by Purbut Singh and his son and heir, Ram Singh, they charged forward in a compact body against the besieging army, directing their attack upon the central point, where the green standard of Mahomet waved above the silken tent of the Padishah. That all might be in a position of equality in the death agony of their race, Purbut Singh and Ram Singh were on foot like the meanest of their followers. The only distinction was, that above the former's head rose the umbrella, symbol of sovereignty, and the Rajput standard with its gold-embroidered imagery indicating the prince's descent from the sun and the moon, dangerous distinctions that would attract in his direction the most determined efforts of the enemy. But after all, as every one of them was bound to die, it was only a question of precedence in the path to *swarga*[1].

The Mahometan lines were protected by an earthen embankment. This was broken through without much resistance at the first onset, as the defenders were taken by surprise. Thus the Rajputs found themselves inside the hostile lines, and hewed their way through the

[1] Swarga = heaven.

camp towards the king's tent. Ahmed Shah hastily mounted the howdah of his state elephant, which formed a rallying centre for the Moslems, driven back by the fury of the Rajputs' first great charge. It took, however, a considerable time before troops from other parts of the besieging lines could assemble at the point of attack, and in the meantime the Padishah, who stood his ground bravely, animating his followers with voice and gesture and occasionally shooting arrows at the advancing Rajputs, was in great danger of death or capture. His body-guard threw themselves in front of his elephant and fought on till almost every one of them fell. Then their place was taken by other forces arriving at the scene of action. Still, the Rajputs were always advancing, although their progress was disputed inch by inch. At last they were right in front of the royal elephant, whose howdah was bristling with the arrows and javelins they had cast at it.

At this point the valour of young Ram Singh nearly consummated Rajput vengeance. He dashed suddenly right under the belly of Ahmed Shah's elephant, and, with his dagger, cut the girths. The howdah toppled over, and the proud Padishah rolled in the dust. One or two of the foremost Rajputs, and Ram Singh himself, pounced upon him like leopards on a deer, but could not manage to kill him. He quickly sprang on his feet sword in hand, and defended himself by his skill in swordsmanship until his nearest followers came in large numbers to the rescue.

Meantime the tide of battle first became stationary and then began slowly to turn, as fresh troops from the more distant parts of the besiegers' lines gradually came up and joined in the fight. In the centre of the camp, to which the Rajputs had advanced in their first furious onset, the Mahometans had closed in upon them on either flank and at last totally surrounded them. Then the Rajputs formed in a circle, defended against the superior numbers of the enemy by no better entrenchment than the dead bodies of the slain. They were now no longer able to advance, and as their numbers grew less and less they had gradually to retire into a more and more contracted circle. Their swords were broken and blunted, and their muscles were becoming exhausted with continual fighting. Thus they were presently compelled for the most part to give up the part of assailants and stand on the defensive. Nevertheless, every now and then small knots of Rajputs would make desperate rushes into the thick of the Moslem ranks, and, after killing as many as they could, meet the death they coveted.

Still Purbut Singh's standard and umbrella of state rose above the dust and the shouting of the conflict, in spite of the most determined efforts of the Mahometans to capture or overthrow it. When Purbut Singh, who through the terrible fight showed the courage of his warlike ancestors, fell pierced with an arrow, and was laid dead among the bodies of his devoted vassals, Ram Singh, as his successor, took his place under the umbrella's shade and renewed the desperate fight for the Rajput standard. When the young prince's sword was broken, he wrested a sharp one from the hands of a burly Khan who had arrived late on the field of battle. With this fresh weapon he slew three foemen, before he himself and the standard with its proud emblems of the Sun and Moon were overthrown. The terrible battle was now finished. The dust settled down on the bodies of five thousand slain, and the Mahometan shouts of

"Din, Din"[1] were no longer re-echoed by the Rajput "Hur, Hur, Mahadev". All the Rajput chivalry of Ahore had perished on the fatal field, but, ere they fell, they had sent an equal or a greater number of their enemies to the shades below.

When Ahmed Shah entered the now undefended fortress to carry off his dearly-won bride he found himself in a city of the dead. Inside, as outside the walls, the whole air reeked with corpses. Here, as on many other occasions, the Rajputs showed that, though they could be killed, they could not be enslaved, and their heroic death, which men and women met with the same unshrinking fortitude, inspired in succeeding generations the unconquerable spirit that secured their liberty against the power of the great Moguls.

II. THE BRIDAL

Ahmed Shah was for a time much depressed in spirits at the tragic results of his wooing. His hopes revived again when he learnt from a spy that the beautiful Lala had, after all, not perished in the holocaust at Ahore. She had

[1] Din = faith.

been secretly conveyed away before the siege and entrusted to the care of a neighbouring chieftain, on whose honour Purbut Singh could depend. When Ahmed Shah heard this he once more demanded the surrender of the girl whom he had determined to make his bride. Purbut Singh's friend was ready to defend her to the last against all the power of the Padishah. But Lala herself refused to be the cause of any further bloodshed. "Since the Padishah is determined to marry me," she exclaimed, "let him have his wish, and may he never repent of its fulfilment!" She not only consented to marry him, but promised to send him costly robes, richly embroidered and decked with many jewels, to wear on his wedding-day. The Rajputs uttered many a deep imprecation on the degenerate girl who thus was willing to marry the exterminator of her race, and become the bride of the man whose hands were red with the blood of her father and brother.

The wedding was to be celebrated on the marble verandah of the Padishah's palace by the Silver Lake. For political as well as personal reasons it was to be a most magnificent ceremony. It was to be a great feast of peace, by which Ahmed Shah hoped not only to gratify his own wishes, but also to unite in harmony the Hindu and the Moslem, so that he might reign over a united kingdom. To further this purpose, an amnesty was proclaimed to all the Rajputs who were then, or had ever been, in rebellion against his rule. The marriage was to be arranged as far as possible in accordance with Hindu customs, and thousands of Brahmins were to be fed on the auspicious occasion. From all parts of his own dominions, and from foreign countries, great crowds assembled to be present on the great day, and all were entertained with kingly hospitality.

Behold Ahmed Shah at last at the summit of his wishes! It is his wedding-day. He and Lala are seated side by side, and the marriage garland hangs around their necks. The lovely bride is clad in bodice and petticoat of the finest silk, and a long white silk scarf, bordered and spotted with red, entwines her waist and is wrapped round her head, which is covered with a triangular head-dress representing a crown. The bridegroom is splendidly attired in the robes, richly embroidered and sparkling with gems, that Lala had sent him as a wedding gift that very morning.

To the disgust of orthodox Mahometans he has taken her hand and a sprig of the sacred basil, and they are now man and wife.

When the ceremony is over, Lala rises gracefully from her seat, and, taking her husband by the hand, leads him to the parapet of the verandah overlooking the Silver Lake. "Let my lord", she says, "stand forth in the sunlight and gladden his loyal subjects with his gracious presence."

As he looked down from this commanding point of view and heard the acclamations of the thousands, clad in holiday attire, who greeted his appearance, it is no wonder that his heart was swollen with pride. The whole lake and its shores were crowded with his subjects, and, far as his eye could reach, he could see no plain, or valley, or mountain that did not belong to his dominions. Above all, he exulted in his beautiful bride, whom he had won from a hostile race after overcoming all opposition by the power of his arms. But she looked strangely into his eyes with a look that was not the timid glance of a young bride, and said solemnly to him, "My lord, enjoy this glorious moment while it lasts. But remember that when men are at the summit of prosperity, they are then most obnoxious to the power of the gods, and we, who are now in the full flush of health, youth, and love, may in a day, nay in an hour, have ceased to be." Ahmed Shah replied with a smile of love and condescension. He was so deeply enamoured of his fair young bride that everything she said or did only made her appear still more lovely in his eyes.

The courtiers on the verandah and the crowds on the lake below watched the fires that seemed to issue from the diamonds on the Padishah's rich vesture as the sun shone upon it. Suddenly, to their surprise and horror they saw a real flame flash from his right shoulder. They could scarcely believe their eyes, but there it was. The heat of the Indian sun had begun to work on the poisonous drugs with which Lala had anointed her bridegroom's robes. Ahmed Shah was a brave man in battle, but in face of the horrible death to which he had been doomed by the woman he loved, he was reduced to the level of ordinary humanity. He shrieked with pain as he rushed to and fro trying to tear the envenomed cloth from his burning flesh. The struggle did not last long. The flames spread over his body with fearful rapidity, and soon nothing was left of the proud Padishah and his rich attire but a gruesome heap of black cinders. In the meantime Lala had calmly mounted the parapet, and, after watching with mingled feelings the death agonies of her bridegroom, and satisfying herself that the death of her father and of her brother, and the destruction of her race, were fully avenged, plunged headlong into the deep waters of the Silver Lake.

The Bond of the Bracelet

IN the durbar-room of a strong hill fortress on the borders of Rajputana a small number of warriors and statesmen, most of them old men, were taking counsel together. On the cushion in the centre sat the old white-bearded Rajah of Nagor, Man Singh. His brow was heavy with care, and all the councillors around him looked equally sad. They had indeed good reason to be melancholy. The rajah's sons, with the greater part of the army of the state, were many hundred leagues away fighting the battles of their suzerain, the Mogul emperor, in the Deccan. During their absence the Mahometan king of Gujarat had suddenly invaded the realms of Nagor with a large army. The old rajah, hopeless of defending his capital, had hurried off with his wives, his daughters, his jewels, such of his chief nobles as were, like himself, too old to go to battle in the Deccan, and a large number of women and children, to the rocky castle of Godwar, leaving the city of Nagor and his marble palace there to the mercy of the foe. The granaries were full of grain, and there was plenty of water in the tanks at Godwar, but the defenders were too few to man properly the extensive ramparts of the strong fortress. The Gujarat army was already beginning to encamp round the walls, and the rajah and his followers in Godwar appeared to have before them only the dismal alternatives of surrender or death. They could not even flee to any other place of refuge if such were available, for the cavalry of the hostile army was already in position, and could easily overtake, surround, and cut them in pieces, even if they succeeded in breaking through the half-formed lines of the besiegers.

Much was said at the council by the wise men there assembled. They discussed the means of holding the castle as long as possible with the scanty forces at their disposal, and whether it was possible to obtain relief from outside. But however much they discussed the matter, they could find no escape from the terrible alternative before them. No neighbouring friendly state was strong enough to offer battle to the large army of Feroze Shah with any hope of success. Whatever way they looked at it, death or surrender stared them in the face. As surrender meant that the princesses of Nagor would be condemned to enter the harem of the Mahometan conqueror, it was determined to perform the terrible ceremony of *johur* rather than suffer such an indignity. In the meantime, however, they resolved first to gain as much time as possible by protracting negotiations for the surrender they never intended to make. After that they would hold the castle to the last, and, if the gods did not drive away the insolent foe, they would, when defence was no longer possible, according to the Rajput ceremony called *johur*, immolate their wives and daughters on the funeral pyre, and then sally forth from the fortress sword in hand, clad in saffron robes, to slay and be slain.

Having come to this conclusion, they returned gloomily to their several apartments, where they were eagerly expected by the women of their families, anxious to know the fate that was in store for them. Among the most eagerly expectant was the Rajah Man Singh's favourite daughter, whose name Punna (the diamond) well expressed the brilliancy of her youthful beauty and the brightness of her intelligence. Though daughters in Rajputana are generally regarded as a burden and an expense, this girl was dearer to the rajah's heart than any of his sons. She was the youngest of his children, the only child of the wife whom he had loved and lost some fourteen years ago, and who for a short time had brightened his declining years. When he looked upon the beauty of Punna, he seemed to see his long-lost wife restored to him from the greedy flames of the funeral pyre. How often he had found solace in his daughter's playfulness and affection when he returned to his palace wearied with the cares of state! How should he now face her with the terrible news he had to tell?

At first he remained silent in the centre of his sorrowing family, who looked to him for comfort with their eyes full of tears. For some time not even the caresses and eager enquiries of his beloved Punna could elicit a reply. At last he summoned resolution to tell them that, unless the gods should come to their assistance, they were all doomed to die at no distant period.

His hearers received the death-warrant in

silence, in tears, or with loud cries of lamentation, according to their different characters and ages. Man Singh's mother, a sybil of nearly a hundred years, proudly, almost eagerly, embraced the opportunity of sealing the devotion of her long life by dying like a true Rajputni. Some of the younger women imitated her high courage, but others were inclined to argue that, as they had more reason to expect pleasure from life, they might naturally be expected to dread death more. The little children, too young to realize what was before them, looked on, as before, with wide-open eyes of wonder at the weeping and wailing of such of their elders as could not refrain from tears.

Punna's attitude on hearing the verdict of death was peculiar and characteristic. She neither looked stern and exalted like the rajah's mother, nor indulged in useless tears like her weaker sisters. She withdrew quietly to a window, the marble trellis-work of which afforded a wide prospect over the surrounding country, and there, with her elbow on the window-sill and her head leaning on her elbow, sat for a while in deep thought. Her eyes at first wandered listlessly over the landscape, until at last they rested on the conical top of a distant mountain just visible in the fading twilight on the verge of the horizon.

Now it was not quite by accident that Punna's eyes found their resting-place on the top of this conical mountain. She was full of imagination, and often in her reveries had built fine castles in the air on the top of the mountain of Arikanda. For there dwelt Umed Singh, a Rajput prince, whose beauty and grace had won her girlish fancy two years before, when as an ally of her father she had seen him ride through the streets of Nagor. He was then almost a boy, and returning with the flush of victory on his brow from an expedition against a strong body of Bhil robbers, in which he had fleshed his maiden sword. As she saw his fair face and the gallant bearing with which he managed his curvetting arab steed, she fell in love with him on the spot, and secretly prayed that, when she married, a young hero like him might be her bridegroom. At the time there seemed no reason why her dream should not become a reality. But the course of true love never did run smooth. It happened that soon after frontier disputes arose between the two neighbouring Rajput states. A bitter and mutual feeling of hostility was the result, which, although it did not break out into open war, put an end to all friendly relations between the two courts. Intermarriage was henceforth out of the question, but this did not prevent Punna from cherishing in her heart the image of the young warrior, who was fixed in her mind for ever as her ideal of manly beauty and courage. Thus it was that in her day-dreams she often fixed her gaze on the mountain of Arikanda, and that even now, when her mind was occupied with far different thoughts, her eyes naturally, by force of custom, turned in that direction.

Suddenly a thought flashed through her brain that made her heart beat fast and her eye brighten with hope. Might she not appeal to her young warrior for help? In this time of terrible need would not the young Rajput forget the petty quarrels that had severed once friendly peoples and come to the aid of a Rajput prince threatened by a Mahometan invader? Why should she not make him her *Rakhi-bund Bhai*, or bracelet-bound brother, binding him to her service by a pledge that no noble Rajput could refuse to accept? For it now happened to be the time of the festival of the bracelet, at which time any Rajput maiden or matron may send a bracelet to whatever cavalier she may choose, and make him her bracelet-bound brother. If the cavalier is willing to accept the gift and its obligations, he sends back to the fair donor a bodice of silk or satin or gold brocade, and is thereafter bound to devote himself like a true knight to her service, and succour her whenever she appeals to him for help in the hour of need.

With such thoughts in her mind she rose and went to her father, who sat with his head in his hands, a picture of hopeless dejection.

"Father," she said, "would you come with me for a moment to the window-recess?"

He followed her listlessly to the place indicated, and as soon as they were out of hearing of the others she said eagerly:

"Has the Prince of Arikanda ever treated you with insolence, or done any base act against you or your subjects that can never be forgiven?"

"No," replied Man Singh, "all his offence against me is that he claims some debatable land on our frontiers that has been a subject of controversy for over a century. The land in question is sandy and barren, and worth nothing to anybody, and perhaps there is some ground for the Arikanda claim to it. But, of course, it would have been a stain on my honour to give up lands held by my father and grandfather whether rightly or wrongly. Thus many angry messages have passed between us, and we were resolved, as soon as your brothers returned from the Deccan, to assert our rights by force of arms. As for the boy himself, he is as gallant a Rajput as ever drew sword, and when he fought on our side against the robber chieftains of the north, I loved him as a son. But why talk of such matters when these cursed Mahometans are encircling our towers and we are all doomed to destruction before the next moon appears?"

"My father," replied Punna, "let me send the bracelet to Umed Singh, and my heart tells me that he will, like a true knight, hurry to our assistance."

"What!" exclaimed Man Singh in a fit of passionate anger. "Shall we humble ourselves to ask help from an enemy, who has defied our power, and whom, but for this Mahometan invasion, we should soon bring to his knees? Perish the thought!"

M 748

"PUNNA WON OVER HER FATHER"

Man Singh was very angry indeed, but Punna knew better than anyone else how to mollify him and bring him round to agree to her proposal, which was, after all, quite reasonable, and was indeed, as far as could be seen, the only hope of safety left. Further, as Rajput princesses had been known to send the bracelet even to Mahometans, there could be no dishonour in Punna's sending her bracelet to a true Rajput prince, although he happened at the time to be an enemy. It was the plain duty of all Rajputs to forget their mutual feuds in the face of the common enemy. Even policy might well urge Umed Singh to come to their assistance. If Nagor were subdued, and became a province of the kingdom of Gujarat, the turn of Arikanda would be likely to come next. Partly by urging such considerations as these, and still more by caresses, Punna won over her father, and it was resolved to send her bracelet by a trusty messenger to Umed Singh.

The bracelet chosen as the symbol of Punna's appeal to the chivalry of Umed Singh was made of gold chains, ornamented with sapphires and diamonds. A boy still in his teens, the son of a trusty old retainer, was selected to perform the difficult and dangerous task of conveying it to Arikanda; and he started at once, so as to get clear before the encircling lines of the leaguer were drawn tight round the fortress walls, and before the morning light made it impossible for the messenger to slip away unseen by the sentries of the enemy.

With many blessings and cautions the brave boy was let down by a rope from the ramparts, and disappeared immediately in the darkness of night. With the swiftness and light step of a mountain deer he threaded his way through the rocky boulders which were scattered over the ground all round the walls of the fortress. The narrow, tortuous paths he trod were so familiar to him that he could follow them easily by the dim light of the stars. But wherever he directed his footsteps, he saw the watch-fires of the foe, separated from each other by no wide intervals. It seemed almost impossible to slip between them undetected. However, the attempt had to be made, and that quickly, for soon the moon would rise and cast her light on the scene. So he made for the middle of the widest interval between the watch-fires, and, keeping as much as possible under the cover of the rocky boulders, managed to escape the eyes of the sentries on both sides. When he had got past the encircling line of fires he hurried on with less caution, thinking that he had now passed the most critical part of his journey. But there's many a slip 'twixt the cup and the lip. Just at this moment a heavy figure sprang upon him from behind a bush at the side of his path, and the two rolled together in the dust. The boy was famous as a clever wrestler in all his boyish sports, but his wiles and struggles were useless against the iron clasp of the strong man who now held him. "No, my little fellow," said his captor, "you must come along with me and pay a visit to the great king of Gujarat in his royal tent."

The boy, finding his struggles useless, resigned, or pretended to resign, himself to his fate, and walked along quietly with the Mahometan, who held him fast by his right arm, and led him in the direction of the nearest watch-fire. In a few minutes he would be searched by the fire-light, and the tell-tale bracelet concealed in his turban would be discovered. Young Banni, however, had by no means given up hope, and was determined to make a bold stroke for liberty even if he perished in the attempt. His captor, lulled into false security by the boy's small size and his apparent submission, foolishly allowed him to have his left arm free, and did not search his clothes to see if he had any weapons concealed about his person. If he had done so, he would have found hidden in his left sleeve a small crooked dagger called a *beechwa* or scorpion, from its resemblance to that venomous reptile. By an adroit movement of his arm Banni managed to get hold of the hilt of his dagger, and immediately plunged its point deep into the fleshy part of the arm of the Mahometan, who yelled with the pain of the sudden wound, and relaxed his hold. Immediately Banni, by a desperate effort, shook himself free and darted away like an arrow, pursued by the Mahometan.

Unfortunately he had shaken himself free not only of the Mahometan's grasp but also of his turban, in the folds of which lay concealed the precious bracelet. He determined if possible to recover it. When his pursuer, floundering along the rocky path, was left some way behind, Banni slipped aside and hid himself behind a boulder. The Mahometan rushed on past him, and Banni quietly and swiftly retraced his steps to the spot where his turban had fallen to the ground. It was lying there still, and Banni, after feeling that the bracelet was still in its place, put the turban on his head and started off once more.

Here an opportunity offered itself, which he was not slow to embrace. The Moslem soldiers round about had been roused by the loud yell of their wounded comrade, that suddenly startled the stillness of the night. Banni could see them peering into the darkness, and wandering about with torches to find out what had happened. A Mahometan officer, richly dressed and mounted on a fine black steed, was riding about and giving orders to the search-parties. Presently, finding his horse rather an encumbrance than a help in the rough jungle, he gave it over to the charge of a small page who was in attendance, and himself went on foot to some distance. Banni was close by when the Mahometan officer gave over his horse to the charge of his page. The horse was restive, and the small page-boy had great difficulty in holding it. As none of the searchers happened to be near, Banni came boldly forward. The page-boy seeing him, called out, "Why don't you come and help me to hold this beast of a horse instead of standing there, you son of a donkey?" Banni was only too glad to accept the offer. He took the bridle in his hand, and said to the page-boy, "If you give me a backsheesh, you can sit down on that stone and I'll hold the horse for you as long as you like." The lazy page-boy upon this left the horse in Banni's hands, and sat down comfortably on a stone to watch another doing his work for him. Banni had not much time to lose. He moved up as if to quiet the horse by patting it on the shoulder, and vaulted lightly into the saddle, without putting his foot in the stirrup.

The page jumped up and gave a loud shout as Banni touched the horse with his heel and rode away swiftly in the direction of Arikanda. Just at this moment the moon rose above a misty cloud low on the eastern horizon. This enabled Banni to ride over the rocky ground with less danger of falling, but it also discovered him, as he rode away, to the eyes of half the encampment of the besiegers. Steeds were mounted in hot haste, and in a few minutes fifty or a hundred troopers were on his track. They had, however, little chance of catching him. For the steed he rode was strong and swift, and his light weight was like a feather on its back. He had soon made his way to the bottom of the rocky hill and was galloping over the great sandy plain between Godwar and Arikanda. Who so proud as he, when he felt the long stride of the great black steed beneath him, bearing him on with the speed of a strong wind and the smooth easy motion of a mighty river! As he looked round he could see by the moonlight his pursuers diminishing in number and becoming dimmer and dimmer in the distance. In front the mountain of Arikanda was clearly visible at a distance of sixty miles, which, as hour followed hour, diminished to fifty, forty, thirty, twenty, and ten miles. At last the black horse began to show signs of exhaustion, and required the aid of the curbed bit to keep him from stumbling. Nevertheless horse and rider struggled on until at dawn they reached the gate of Arikanda, which had just been opened to admit the country people bringing provisions into the town.

Banni was immediately conducted, in accordance with his request, to the royal palace, in the court-yard of which he found a splendid cavalcade with hawk and hound preparing to start for the greenwood. In the centre of the group were two tall young men attired in hunting dress, one of whom was pointed out to him as Umed Singh, the chief of Arikanda. Banni immediately slipped down from his horse, ran forward to him, and put in his hands the bracelet, telling him that it was sent by Punna, who with her father was shut up by a Mahometan army in Godwar, and called upon him as a true Rajput cavalier to come to her assistance. Umed Singh's brow flushed with pride. He felt it a high honour that the peerless Punna should have made such an appeal to him in spite of the hostility that had existed for some years between the two states.

"I have nobler game afoot," he exclaimed to his companion, "than heron, deer, or tiger. Feroze Shah is besieging Man Singh in his fortress of Godwar, and his fair daughter Punna has given me the honour of coming to her assistance as her brother, bound to her by the bond of the bracelet. So, my friend, I must bid you farewell and go to the wars."

"And why farewell?" said the other. "If Punna is now your adopted sister, Zalim Singh is your brother-in-arms, and, with the fifty knights who have so long been enjoying your hospitality, will be proud to fight under your flag at Godwar."

The retainers of both princes raised a hearty cheer when they heard Zalim Singh express this generous resolution, and the word was sent round to prepare for war with all possible speed. In the meantime Banni and the good horse that carried him so well were not forgotten. Refreshment was provided for man and beast, and Banni, the hero of the hour, had to relate over and over again all that he had done and suffered since he slid down the rope from the ramparts of Godwar.

In the meantime Feroze Shah had begun to attack Godwar, without waiting for the arrival of his heavy guns, which were two or three days' march behind the rest of his army. On the very morning on which Banni so cleverly made his way to Arikanda an attempt was made to scale the walls before daybreak. A native of the place, who had turned traitor, undertook to climb up the rocks by a path known only to himself, and let down a rope-ladder. A strong forlorn hope waited at the foot of the almost precipitous rock until the lower end of the rope came dangling down to the ground on which they were standing, and assured them of the traitor's success. Their satisfaction, however, was short-lived. Almost before the first of them had set foot on the lowest rung, the whole ladder was suddenly jerked up, and down came rolling a round object like a ball, which turned out, on inspection, to be the head of the traitor. He had been detected in the act of fastening the ladder to the top of the ramparts by the sentries, who promptly leaped upon him, and, cutting off his head, threw it down over the wall.

On the following day the besiegers were busy constructing mines and trenches. The small garrison could do little or nothing to obstruct these operations, as feint attacks were made at different parts of the wide circuit of the walls, which, although they were not pressed home, had to be opposed. No serious attempt was made to scale the walls. The besiegers preferred to wait for the arrival of their heavy guns. They had no doubt that, when these arrived and were directed against the walls by the skilled Portuguese gunners from Diu in Feroze's service, a practicable breach would soon be effected and the fortress would fall. In the middle of the night a runner climbed the wall bearing a *katchli* or bodice of gold brocade and pearls for Punna from Umed Singh, who thereby acknowledged the receipt of the bracelet, and declared his willingness to accept all the obligations implied in the gift. Hope rose still higher when it was heard that Zalim Singh was going to join his forces with those of Umed Singh, and march with him to Godwar.

As Umed Singh and Zalim Singh rode together at the head of the whole army of the former and the fifty knights of the latter, they consulted together on the situation of affairs. As they had only about 5000 troopers, and the army besieging Godwar was at least three times that number, it would not be wise to offer battle. They resolved rather to hover round the besieging army, and watch for any opportunity of throwing in reinforcements. Above all, their best plan was to cut the communications of the enemy, who were in a barren and hostile country, and would find it very difficult to get their supplies from Gujarat.

So they moved rapidly to the south-west of Godwar and took up a strong position commanding the main road from Ahmedabad, the capital of Gujarat.

They had hardly established themselves there when a Rajput came galloping into the camp with the news that the Mahometan artillery was approaching with a slender escort, and that the officers in command seemed to be taking no precautions against surprise. Umed Singh immediately advanced to meet them with 2000 of his troopers, whom he concealed on either side of a defile through which the road passed. Presently the artillery appeared in sight, moving on slowly, the guns dragged by the large bullocks for which the province of Gujarat is famous. The few horsemen who rode in front as an advance guard were allowed to pass through the defile unmolested. Not until the guns in charge of the Portuguese artillerymen were right between the two lines of the Rajput ambush was the order given for the attack. Then a mingled hail of bullets and arrows from an unseen foe poured into the ranks of the doomed gunners, who discharged their muskets wildly without doing much damage. The confusion was increased by the rushing to and fro of the great oxen, some of whom were accidentally wounded by the Rajput discharge. The attack was so sudden and unexpected, and the force attacked was so small, that resistance was hopeless. So the Portuguese gunners and their small escort were compelled to surrender after a considerable number of them had fallen. The Rajput leaders did not think they were strong enough to hold the guns they had captured. They would have been a serious encumbrance, and would have interfered with their superior mobility, by which they hoped to make up for their inferior numbers. So they threw the captured artillery into a neighbouring tank, and with the Portuguese prisoners and the oxen retired to their original position, which was already threatened by a large force detached from the besieging army. They had good reason to be well satisfied with what they had done. Feroze Shah deprived of his artillery would have little chance of speedily effecting the capture of Godwar now that he had an active force operating in his rear. The moral effect of the blow was also very considerable. The Gujaratis were dispirited to find that instead of carrying all before them, they were themselves opposed to attack, and they began to fear that many of them might perish in the sandy plains of Rajputana and never see the rich pastures of their native land again.

On the other hand, the spirits of the Rajputs were proportionately elevated. The news of the capture of the artillery was spread by rumour far and wide over the country. The Rajputs of the neighbouring states prepared to take part in what promised to be a successful resistance to a Mahometan invasion. From the territory of Nagor also, by twos and threes and fours, Rajput warriors came riding in to swell the ranks of the relieving force. Most of the latter, it is true, were old men or boys, as almost all the men of military age were away fighting in the Deccan under the imperial standard. But still their presence was a very welcome addition to the still scanty numbers of the little army under Umed Singh's command.

In the meantime the army of Feroze Shah was reduced to a position of considerable difficulty. Owing to the severing of its communications, provisions were beginning to run short. The only way to remedy this trying state of affairs was to storm the walls of Godwar and gain access to the large stores known to have been there collected. A mine was successfully exploded under the bastion protecting the approach to the main gateway, and up the débris of the broken masonry clambered the valiant Moslem soldiery, shouting their religious war cry, "Din, Din!"[1] which was answered by the defenders of the breach with loud shouts of defiance. The explosion of the mine warned the relieving army of the danger that threatened the beleaguered garrison. Umed Singh immediately drew out his cavalry in battle array, and directed the main body against the Moslem lines immediately in the rear of the storming party. This diversion compelled Feroze Shah to turn against the enemy on the outside the troops that he had massed for the support of the soldiers attacking the breach. At the same time Zalim Singh with his fifty knights rode swiftly round the lines, threatening them at different points in quick succession, and driving his attack home wherever he found the long circuit of the lines weakly defended. Owing to these diversions the attempt to

[1] Faith, Faith!

storm the breach had to be abandoned, and after a good deal of desultory fighting, in which no decisive success was gained on either side, both parties retired to their respective camps.

Feroze Shah saw from the ineffectual result of the day's fighting that he could not expect to gain possession of Godwar unless he could inflict a decisive defeat on Umed Singh. Indeed, unless he could do so and restore his communications with Gujarat, there was great danger that his army, though unconquered in the field, would be reduced by starvation. He therefore determined on the following day to direct his main attack upon the Rajput position on the road to Ahmedabad, leaving a small containing force to prevent the garrison of Godwar from sallying and making an attack in his rear in the heat of the battle. Early in the morning the Mahometan army advanced to battle with the main body of infantry in the centre, and squadrons of cavalry on either wing. Feroze Shah himself took up his position, surrounded by his body-guard, in the rear of his advancing troops, where he was to be seen seated on the howdah of a richly-caparisoned elephant, with the umbrella, the oriental symbol of sovereignty, held over his head. The Rajputs with their inferior numbers could hardly hope to defeat this powerful and well-ordered force in a pitched battle. If they hurled themselves on the spears of the Mahometan infantry in the centre, they would be in danger of being attacked on both flanks by the cavalry arrayed on the right and left wings of the enemy's line of battle. Umed Singh was wise as he was brave, and saw clearly that if he made a frontal attack on the advancing enemy he would be courting defeat. He therefore determined to follow Parthian tactics, and conquer by retreating. As soon as the enemy advanced to within bow-shot, the Rajputs delivered a volley from their matchlocks and bows, and then retired in good order to a new position farther back. By repeating these tactics several times, they lured the Mahometan army farther and farther away from Godwar. Then the counterstroke was delivered. The next time the Mahometan army came within striking distance, all the Rajputs suddenly, like one man, took a half-turn to the right. The main body, consisting of some 4000 men led by Zalim Singh, hurled itself on the cavalry arrayed on the Mahometan left, and after a short but desperate struggle drove them back on the centre. The victorious Rajputs, excited by their success, now did what their leaders never intended them to do. They charged the Mahometan infantry, and, as was to be expected, failed to pierce the impenetrable forest of their spears. Not till they had lost many men in fruitless charges, and were threatened in their turn by a flank attack from the Gujarati cavalry, who had ridden round from the right wing, could Zalim Singh prevail upon them to retire. Their leader, with his own band of fifty knights, or what had originally been fifty knights, kept the advancing Mahometan cavalry in check until the whole of the main body of Rajputs was able to extricate itself from the perilous position in which its rash valour had involved it. Before, however, this could be done the blood of many a gallant horse and rider stained the sand.

In the meantime a chosen band of a thousand warriors, under the command of Umed Singh, had fetched a compass round the turmoil and confusion of the fight, and made straight for the main gate of Godwar castle. As Man

Singh and Punna looked down from their favourite post of observation, a turret rising high above the eastern ramparts, they saw the battle raging in the distance. At first they could only see one cloud of dust, here and there illuminated by the rays of the newly-risen sun flashing on sword, shield, and helmet. Then a smaller cloud of dust detached itself from the main body, and was seen to move rapidly in the direction of Godwar. What could it be? Was it a body of routed Moslem cavalry that had fled from the battle and left the infantry to its fate, or was it a company of Rajputs that had given up the battle for lost and was making for Arikanda and safety? Soon the keenly-interested spectators saw the flag of five colours flying above the advancing squadron, and knew thereby that it consisted of Rajputs. Next they could make out the special flag of the state of Arikanda, and Punna concluded that the troop of horse was commanded by her adopted brother. Her heart told her that he was no traitor or run-away, and soon all the spectators saw that his object was to force his way through the beleaguering lines into the fortress. The Mahometans in the besieging lines saw it too, and began to concentrate in front of the gates to oppose his advance.

Umed Singh paused for a few moments before giving the order to charge. "They shrink from the onset!" cried the Mahometan commander. "Advance, my men, and break through their wavering ranks!" Umed Singh, however, was not at all inclined to shrink from the onset. He was only giving his horses and men a moment's breathing space, that their charge might be the more effective. Then the rocky ground resounded to the tread of four thousand hoofs, and almost in a moment, as it seemed, the front line of the enemy was broken. The second line made a longer resistance, until they were driven back under the walls and were assailed by great stones, arrows, and javelins hurled down on their heads from the ramparts. Thus exposed to a double attack in front and in rear they could sustain the fight no longer, but broke and fled. The great gate was then opened, and into Godwar rode the victorious squadron, bearing with them their dead and wounded. The common soldiers of the garrison crowded round to kiss the feet of Umed Singh, whom they greeted as their deliverer.

Not less warm was the welcome which he received from Man Singh and his nobles. The due meed of praise and glory was also given to Banni, who rode in with Umed Singh's troopers on the great black horse he had seized on his adventurous passage through the beleaguering lines.

Thus it was that when Feroze Shah returned on his elephant to his tent in the centre of his encampment, after defeating and driving before him the main body of the Rajputs, he found that all the fruits of victory were with the enemy. The Rajputs who remained outside were not cast down by the repulse they had sustained, and were still in sufficient numbers to intercept his communications. He also knew that they would soon be strongly reinforced by large bands of Rajputs who were moving to the scene of action. As there was no lack of water or provisions, the garrison of Godwar, with the additional thousand men thrown in by Umed Singh, could now, in all probability, successfully defend the walls until Man Singh's sons returned from the imperial campaign in the Deccan.

Under the circumstances, Feroze Shah thought it expedient to give up the siege.

He therefore invited Umed Singh to a parley, and proposed terms of peace. He especially demanded a solemn promise that his army should be unmolested on its retreat. When the Rajput was inclined to reject this demand, he said, "Very well, unless you swear by all you hold sacred that you will abstain from attacking us on our march, we shall first direct our steps to the city of Nagor, which we have hitherto spared, and, when we have left it, you will not find one stone standing on another." This threat to destroy Man Singh's capital was effectual. Feroze Shah was granted an unmolested retreat, and marched away with his army on the following morning.

Great was the rejoicing in Godwar when the mighty king of Gujarat marched away. Man Singh, as he watched the invading army depart, again and again expressed to Umed Singh his gratitude for the chivalry with which he had hastened to the assistance of the beleaguered fortress, and his admiration of the valour and skill with which the enterprise had been conducted to a successful conclusion. "What recompense", he exclaimed, "can I make you for saving the lives and the honour of myself, my wives, and my daughters? Ask what you will, and I cannot refuse you, though you should demand this castle of Godwar or the most precious gems in my diadem." "Rajah," replied Umed Singh, "I take you at your word, and ask you to give me the priceless diamond that is the greatest glory of your palace and kingdom." Man Singh thought he meant the great diamond that blazed in the centre of his regal tiara, and had descended to him from a long line of ancestors. "You shall have it," he replied; "and long may it remain with your descendants as a symbol of one of the greatest feats of Rajput chivalry!" Umed Singh, however, went on to explain that the diamond he coveted was Man Singh's beautiful daughter Punna, whose name, as we have seen, signified a diamond. Man Singh gladly granted this request, for, as he jokingly remarked, the diamond would not be entirely lost to him by being given to Umed Singh. Punna, by becoming Umed Singh's wife, would not cease to be his daughter. So Umed Singh and Punna were married amid the rejoicings of all Nagor and Arikanda. All the Rajput chiefs who came to the assistance of Godwar before or after the retreat of Feroze Shah were invited to Nagor to grace the wedding with their presence. And there, in Man Singh's marble palace, with due rites and the singing of sacred hymns, and with the clash of arms when the bridegroom rushed in, according to the Rajput custom, with his band of armed kinsmen to go through the form of capturing the bride, Punna gave up her position as adopted sister, and became the wedded wife of Umed Singh. By the help of Romesh Dutt's recent translation into English verse of the great Indian epic of the Ramayana, we can well imagine how Umed Singh took his fair bride back with him to Arikanda—

> "And they reached the ancient city, decked with banners bright and brave,
> And the voice of drum and trumpet hailed the home-returning brave;
> Fragrant blossoms strewed the pathway, song of welcome filled the air,
> Joyous men and merry women issued forth in garments fair;
> And they lifted up their voices, and they waved their hands on high,
> And they raised the voice of welcome as their valiant prince drew nigh".

A Rajput Amazon

SOME four hundred years ago a tall and powerful young Rajput was riding through the glades of a forest on the lower slopes of the Aravalli Mountains. The classic regularity of his features and the smallness of his hands and feet indicated pretty plainly that the bluest blood of Rajasthan flowed in his veins. Though the territory under his rule was not very extensive, Pertab Singh could trace his pedigree back to Rama, the great conqueror of Ceylon, whose exploits were celebrated in immortal verse as old as, or older than, the Iliad and Odyssey. He was clad in the garb of a hunter, and held a lance in his hand, ready for any wild beast that he might encounter.

He had ridden for several hours without getting any sport, when at last he descried a mighty boar in the distance. After an exciting chase, rendered very dangerous by the roughness of the ground and the trees through which he had to guide his horse, he came upon the quarry and drove his spear into its side. Unfortunately, just at this moment his horse put its foot in a hole and fell, throwing its rider in the dust. In the sudden fall the boar-spear snapped, and half of it remained sticking in the animal's side.

Pertab Singh immediately sprang to his feet sword in hand and prepared to defend himself against the boar. The savage animal, rather enraged than weakened by the spear in its side, rushed at him furiously, gnashing its teeth and raising the bristles on its brawny back. Now the boar is the bravest, and one of the strongest, of the beasts of the jungle, and a short sword is a poor defence against his terrible tusks. How Pertab Singh would have fared in the contest with his wounded enemy can never be known. Just at the moment when man and beast were closing in deadly combat, the latter suddenly and mysteriously rolled over and expired.

When Pertab Singh, thus released from imminent peril, proceeded to examine the dead beast, he found the cause of its sudden overthrow to be an arrow from an unseen hand that had sunk up to the feather in its body.

Looking round to discover who had so opportunely come to his assistance, he saw framed in the overarching foliage of two great forest trees a vision of loveliness that almost took his breath away. Seated on a prancing Arab steed, that seemed proud of his beautiful burden, was a young girl of some fifteen or sixteen summers with a bow in her hands.

Had Pertab Singh been a Greek, he might have thought that the figure before him was the goddess Diana come down from Olympus to save her votary from death. Her girlish beauty was enhanced by the brightness of her complexion, due to a healthy life in the open air, and if her soft cheek was slightly browned by exposure to the sun, that too, in Pertab Singh's eyes, made her far more attractive than any of the pale-faced beauties of the zenana. Every motion and pose of her supple form was full of grace, and horse and rider in their perfect harmony formed such a combination of living loveliness as Pertab Singh's eyes had never seen before. But the vision was as transitory as it was enchanting. Before Pertab Singh had recovered from his surprise, the girl turned her horse's head and disappeared in the greenery of the forest with the rapidity of a startled fawn. But for the arrow buried deep in the side of the dead boar, he might have thought the fair maiden and her horse to be creatures of his imagination.

By this time the sun was riding high in the heavens, and Pertab Singh, who had ridden out early in the morning, was becoming hungry and thirsty. He therefore mounted his horse and followed a clearly-marked path, which he hoped might lead him to human habitations. In this hope he was not disappointed. After following the path into one of the most secluded glades of the great forest, he found before him a small settlement of huts which seemed to have been newly erected. Approaching the large hut in the centre, he was told it was the temporary home of the Rajput Ajit Singh, who had been driven from his city and lands by the Afghan Daud.

Pertab Singh was welcomed with courteous hospitality by the expatriated prince. After his body and soul had been refreshed with the best of woodland cheer, he told his host who he was and how he had been saved from the onset of the boar by a beautiful huntress, who had fled from his gaze almost as soon as he had set eyes on her.

"The girl you describe", replied Ajit Singh, "can be none other than my madcap daughter, Pudmani. Since we were expelled from our castle by the Afghans she has been roaming the forest like a wild woman, and has attained wonderful skill with the bow and arrow. The spoiled child declares that, now that she has once tasted the joys of free life in the forest, she will never submit to be immured in the pale shade of the zenana. Indeed she is so self-willed that I know not what to do with her."

"If one so lovely", replied the gallant young Rajput, "would deign to look with favour on me, I would be her willing slave for life, and my chief joy and pride would be to satisfy every wish of her heart."

"Truly, as I look on you, I see that you are not such a one as maidens are wont to frown upon. But here is another of my Pudmani's freaks of fancy. She swears she will marry no one who cannot win back our ancestral city and castle from Daud the Afghan, and whoever does this, she will marry, be he as black as a negro and as ugly as a rakshasa[1]."

"With gladness of heart", replied Pertab

[1] Rakshasa = demon.

Singh, "I undertake the enterprise, and swear to regain your castle of Rajgurh or die in the attempt."

On the same day another offer of marriage for Pudmani came from a very different and most unexpected quarter. The report of her beauty had come to the ears of Daud the Afghan, who, although he was somewhat declined in the vale of years and had two Mahometan wives already, proposed to add the fair Rajputni[1] to their number. He therefore sent a trusty messenger to Ajit Singh's forest home with a letter in which he declared his passion. The lovely Pudmani, he wrote, whose face was like the moon, whose eyes were stars, whose teeth were strings of pearls, the breath of whose coral lips was as the odour of myrrh and camphor, whose form was light and graceful as the gazelle, would henceforth be the sovereign of his heart. Let her therefore come and share his heart and his domains. The letter concluded in a less pleasant strain with a threat that if the proffered honour were declined, he would enter the forest with sword and spear and carry off Pudmani by force.

Ajit Singh was so furiously angry at Daud's

[1] Rajputni = Rajput woman.

letter that he was very much inclined to cut the messenger's head off. He rushed off in a rage to the apartment of his daughter, who was almost as angry as himself at Daud's insolence. When he had ceased fuming at the Afghan's letter, he told Pudmani of the more eligible suitor who had applied for her hand.

Then an idea flashed into her quick brains. "Let us allow the messenger's head to remain on his shoulders for the present," she exclaimed. "One of my admirers is old, short, and fat; the other is young, tall, and handsome. Yet I seem to see a way by which both their proposals may lead to your restoration to your ancestral home and honours. Let us meet and consider the matter with the young gallant who would fight his way into Rajgurh for my sake."

So a council of war was held, the result of which was that a message was sent back to Daud informing him that his offer was accepted, and that in the course of a month Pudmani would be sent to him with a retinue befitting her high rank. At the same time, lest too ready compliance should excite suspicions, it was stipulated that Daud should solemnly swear on the Koran to restore a certain part of Ajit Singh's territory. Daud was so enamoured of the reputed beauty of Pudmani that he could refuse nothing. So on these terms the matter was settled, seemingly to the satisfaction of all concerned.

A month later a gallant cavalcade accompanied Pudmani on her way from her father's forest retreat to the town and fortress of Rajgurh. In the centre Pudmani was carried in a litter, with curtains of white silk. Immediately behind was her beautiful Arab horse led by a groom, who, on close examination, might be seen to be none other than the Rajput prince, Pertab Singh. On either side of the central litter were three litters purporting to be occupied by six ladies-in-waiting, who were to attend upon Pudmani in her new home. Their real occupants were six Rajput warriors, and among the cushions were concealed swords and javelins. Each of the seven litters was borne by six bearers, who were not ordinary *bhois*[1], but warriors in disguise. Thus, not counting Pudmani herself, who had her unerring bow and arrows by her side, there was a masked force of forty-nine Raj-

[1] Bhois = palanquin-bearers.

puts in the seemingly peaceful procession. To this must be added the undisguised guard-of-honour, consisting of thirty troopers. Most of them carried two swords, but as this was a common practice among the Rajputs, it was not likely to attract suspicious attention.

This formidable body of desperate men, all the more formidable because they appeared in festive guise, advanced boldly to Rajgurh. A mile or two from the gates they were met by Daud the Afghan and some twenty of his relatives and friends, all mounted on gallant steeds and robed in festive attire. Daud himself, who was something of a dandy, was arrayed in bright-coloured garments skilfully contrived to conceal the rotundity of his figure. He managed his prancing steed with the address of an accomplished horseman, and Pudmani, as she looked at him through the curtains of the litter, could not but admire the gallant bearing of her elderly admirer. He was indeed a famous warrior, who had fought valiantly in a hundred battles and sieges since the time when he first bore a sword.

The great gates of Rajgurh were thrown wide open to admit the bridal cortege. Directly the threshold was crossed, the carefully-prepared transformation scene was enacted. The seven litters were deposited on the ground. Out of the central one sprang Pudmani, her bow in her hand, and mounted on her Arab steed, which Pertab Singh held ready for her. At the same time some of the disguised Rajputs supplied themselves with weapons from the litters, while others took the extra swords from the troopers forming the guard-of-honour. On the other side, Daud, quickly recovering from his surprise, drew up his small troop of horsemen in battle array behind him, and ordered the trumpeter to sound an alarm and rouse the rest of the Mahometan garrison. Many of the spectators of the strange scene, who had come in festive robes, as for a peaceful procession, rushed to seize arms. Some of these were Mahometan soldiers and settlers, but others belonged to the old Hindu population of the town, and were ready to fight for their liberty and religion.

The fray was opened by Pudmani. As soon as she had mounted her Arab, she put an arrow to the string of her bow and aimed it at the heart of Daud. Then by a sudden change of mind, due no doubt to the tenderness most women feel for even the least acceptable men who honour them with their admiration, she depressed the point of her arrow and shot his horse instead. Her momentary tenderness almost proved fatal to the whole enterprise. Daud rolled in the dust with his wounded horse, but soon picked himself up again. When he looked round, the Rajputs were driving the Afghans back, and in the excitement of victory pursuing them into the interior of the town. He saw the mistake they had made, and with admirable promptitude and presence of mind, instead of going to the scene of conflict where his single arm would have availed little, he ran to the gates, which were now clear of the combatants, and with his own hand helped the gate-keepers to close them. If he had succeeded in his attempt, the small band of Rajputs in the town, deprived of all hope of succour, would have perished like rats in a trap, and Pudmani would, after all, have become an inmate of a Mahometan harem. He was, however, just a moment too late. Before the two heavy halves of the gate met, the foremost of a strong body of Rajputs that had been collected within sight of the walls, ready to enter the town as soon as the pretended bridal party had effected a lodgment, appeared on the scene, and forced their way in through the gate to the help of their comrades.

When Daud was foiled in this attempt he mounted a riderless horse and put himself at the head of the garrison, that had by this time turned out in its full strength and almost surrounded the small body of Rajputs led by Pertab Singh. The Rajput prince performed prodigies of valour; but he was wounded, and many of his bravest comrades had fallen by his side. In their midst rose conspicuous the beautiful form of Pudmani on horseback dealing death from her unerring bow. Like the gleam of a sail to shipwrecked mariners was the appearance of the reinforcements that now began to pour in through the open gates. When all the Rajputs had made their way inside the town, and were joined by the Hindu residents, the Mahometans began to be overpowered by superior numbers. The indomitable Daud made a last effort to retrieve the fortunes of the day by attacking the leader of the enemy. On horseback he made for Pertab Singh, who, slipping aside and evading the weight of the charging horse, caught him by the middle, and by main force pulled him out of the saddle. When Daud was thus captured, his dispirited followers gave up the struggle and asked for quarter, which was granted them.

Thus Pertab Singh won Pudmani for himself, and Rajgurh for her father. Daud owed his life to the pleading of Pudmani. He was more in love with Pudmani than ever now that he had seen her with his own eyes, and he had the gallantry to remark aloud that the sight of her radiant beauty was enough to compensate him for the loss of castle and lands. To himself he swore that he would one day carry her off by force of arms, and have her for his bride after all. This he did not effect, although he lived for many years, and distinguished himself by his skill and valour in more battles and sieges.

Pertab Singh and Pudmani were blessed with a large family. As might be expected from their parentage, the daughters were beautiful and the sons became valiant men, who in the next generation stood forth as bulwarks of the liberty of Rajasthan against the ever-encroaching waves of Mahometan aggression.

The Ruby of Hazrat

IN the spring of 1526 Mukarrab Khan, the younger brother of the Mogul chief of Hazrat, a small state in the country now called Afghanistan, was returning home from a distant embassy. Followed by his half-dozen followers, he rode fast, not stopping by the way to make enquiries, and did not draw rein till he reached his brother's fortress on the outskirts of the town of Hazrat.

The fortress appeared strangely quiet; but the quiet was not that of peace, for when he approached the principal gate he found it smashed in pieces and hanging idly on its hinges. Full of alarm, he dismounted from his horse and hurried in, sword in hand. There was no enemy to dispute his passage, but wherever he looked he saw death and devastation. The tapestry and ornamental wood-work of the rooms had been destroyed and torn down, and broken boxes lay here and there. On the floors men, women, and children were weltering in their blood.

In an upper room, surrounded by the dead bodies of faithful vassals, lay his brother's wife with her murdered infant by her side. Her own dagger plunged in her bosom showed that she had sought and found death by her own hands. Her bracelets, ear-rings, and other ornaments had been violently torn from her. Mukarrab Khan stood aghast at the sickening scene, and long looked in vain for a living being who could explain all the horrors that he saw before him.

At last, from a corner of the room, where he had long lain unconscious, staggered a white-bearded mullah[1], well known to him as the oldest and most devoted adherent of his race. Three of the fingers of his right hand were cut off, and he was so deeply wounded in the side that he was evidently on the point of death. However, he found breath to tell the terrible tale of what had happened, though his words were often interrupted by gasps and sobs.

He related how the chief of Hazrat had marched out with almost all his followers to meet a powerful enemy, and how he had fallen into an ambush and perished

[1] Mahometan priest.

with the whole of his small army. Immediately the news of this terrible disaster reached Hazrat, Mansur, the leader of a large band of robbers, had swooped down from the mountains on the fortress. The few soldiers left to guard it had made a valiant defence, but had been overpowered by numbers. The robbers, after plundering every room in the fortress, had drawn off with their booty to their mountain fastness. "But there is one thing that they have not got," he added, "though they sought for it in every nook and cranny—the ruby of the house of Hazrat. Before the last fatal assault was made, your brother's wife slipped it into my hand, hoping that the murderous dogs might spare me as a man of God. Though almost done to death, I have managed to keep it safe, and now hand it over to you, as the sole survivor and heir of the house, to whose service I devoted my life and in whose service I die." And in fact, as he handed over the priceless gem to Mukarrab Khan, his eyes began to glaze, and he fell down dead.

Mukarrab Khan hastily thrust the gem into his waistband and came outside the house, where five of his followers were waiting for him. He was told that the sixth had followed him into the fortress, and, coming out again immediately before him, had suddenly got on horseback and ridden off in the direction of the mountains. Mukarrab Khan immediately suspected his absent trooper of treachery, and prepared for the worst. In case immediate flight should prove necessary, he directed some of the townspeople, who had in the meantime assembled, to perform the last offices in honour of the dead, if he were compelled himself to leave the spot, and told his remaining troopers to bait their horses and to be ready to mount and ride away at a moment's notice.

We must now follow the steps of the deserter, who had seen and heard all that passed between Mukarrab Khan and the priest, and was resolved either to gain possession of the ruby of Hazrat for himself, or, at any rate, to make as much as possible out of the knowledge he had obtained.

With this intention he rode off in the direction of the mountains, thinking he could best carry out his treacherous project by associating himself with the band of robbers who had sacked the fortress of Hazrat. Fortune was kind to him. Before he had ridden many miles he fell into an ambush of those very robbers, and was led before their chieftain, a black-bearded Afghan, with a chest like a gorilla, and mounted on a clumsy-looking but very powerful black steed of the Turkoman breed.

On being interrogated, the traitor declared that he had secret information which he would communicate to none but the chieftain. The inferior robbers were therefore ordered to stand aloof, and he was told to say quickly what he had to say.

"I know", he said, "where the ruby of Hazrat is, and if you and your band will help me to get it, I will divide a thousand rupees among you."

"You offer little", scornfully replied the bandit, "for the use of our good swords, and for the possession of such a gem as does not shine in the diadem of the Shah of Persia or the Sultan of Rum."

This was the beginning of an animated haggling contest between the two villains, in which the bandit insisted that, as he provided the necessary force, he alone should possess the precious gem. At last a bargain was struck, by which Mukarrab Khan's treacherous trooper was to receive fifty gold pieces on the spot. He was then to reveal the secret, and was to receive a hundred more gold pieces when the gem was won. Accordingly, as the first step towards the fulfilment of the terms of the bargain, the robber produced from a leathern belt round his waist fifty gold coins, and handed them over to the other party. His informant then told him that the gem was in the hands of Mukarrab Khan, who was even then at Hazrat.

"I have paid you in advance fifty gold pieces," replied the bandit, placing his right hand carelessly behind his back, "for your information, and now I must reward you for your treachery to your chief. So perish all", he continued in a loud voice for the benefit of his own followers, "who do the like again." So saying, with a battle-axe that was slung behind him he clove the traitor through his turban to the chin. He then coolly took back from the hands of the dead man the price of his treachery, after which, leaving the corpse to the vultures, he ordered his followers to mount, and at their head rode rapidly down towards Hazrat.

Thus it was that, before he had done giving

directions about the burial of the dead, Mukarrab Khan saw riding down from the mountains a troop of thirty horsemen. He shrewdly guessed what had happened, and knew that he was betrayed. So he mounted his horse, and told his five men to do the same. As they had all been prepared for a sudden flight by Mukarrab Khan's foresight, there was hardly a moment's delay, and they thus managed to get a good start of their pursuers.

Mukarrab Khan made for a pass leading to the south, hoping, if fortune favoured him, to make his way to Kabul, where the enterprising Babar then held sway. He and his five followers had no difficulty in reaching the entrance to the pass before their enemies. Then pursued and pursuers swept along the stony way through the pass. The bandit chief, on his great black Turkoman horse, was so far in front of his followers that he seemed a kind of connecting link between the two parties. It was a race for life and death. The horse of one of Mukarrab Khan's men slipped on a loose stone and fell with its rider. Immediately the two bodies—the man and the horse—as they lay in the narrow way, were spurned by a hundred hoofs; for the robbers rode over them, not waiting to strip the fallen trooper of his arms, as they knew that the prince, conspicuous in his scarlet robe and shining Persian mail, was their quarry.

Without other incident, the two parties of horsemen traversed the pass and emerged in the open plain to the southward. Here Mukarrab Khan ordered his five remaining followers to leave him. This was evidently the best course to adopt for their safety and his own. He was mounted on an Arab of the purest breed, whose swiftness he had to restrain as long as he wished to keep in the company of his followers, who were mounted on ordinary country-bred horses. Also, he knew well that the ruby which he had in his waistband was the sole object of the robbers' determined pursuit. All this flashed through his mind in the tumultuous rush through the pass. The result answered his expectations. When his five men parted from him and took a different route over the plain, they were left to proceed on their way in peace, and the whole body of pursuers, headed by the great black horse of the robber chieftain, followed the track of Mukarrab Khan's Arab steed.

Directly Mukarrab Khan found himself alone, he gave the reins to his horse, which immediately scoured the soft green sward with the speed of lightning, tossing its mane triumphantly, and rejoicing to be at last free from the constraint of the tightened rein. This sudden rush considerably widened the interval between the Mogul prince and his pursuers, although the black steed of the robber chief nobly responded to his master's call, and soon left far behind the smaller horses on which the other robbers were mounted. In this way, after a few hours, the position of affairs entirely changed, until, when the sun began to sink below the horizon, the contest of speed and endurance was confined to the beautiful light-footed chestnut Arab and the heavy Turkoman horse, all baser competitors having entirely disappeared, except two or three that were still dimly visible on the northern horizon, plodding on wearied and hopeless.

It was likely that, barring accidents, the chestnut would win. The black horse, for all its bone and muscle, was beginning to feel the weight of the heavy armour and heavy rider on its back. To lessen this disadvantage the robber recklessly cast away not only his horseman's cloak, but also his heavy breast-plate and head-piece, hoping that if it came to a single combat he could easily, even without their protection, overcome such a slender stripling as Mukarrab Khan appeared to be. Even so the interval between the two horses was not sensibly diminished, and the bandit began to feel that he would be balked of his prey.

Just at this juncture Mukarrab Khan looked round, and saw that only one of his pursuers was near him. The warlike spirit of his race, and anger at the indignity of having had to flee so far and so fast, made him resolve to turn and face his enemy. He therefore slackened speed, and, taking his bow in his hand, drew an arrow from his quiver. Then he suddenly pulled up his horse and turned to face his pursuer, with an arrow on the bow-string. The burly Afghan on his great horse came thundering on, and now, painfully conscious of the want of the defensive armour that he had thrown away, bent down over his horse's head, so as to present as small a mark as possible to the coming missile. The arrow whizzed through the air. It missed the man, but struck the animal on the shoulder. The horse reared, and the rider, to the surprise and delight of Mukarrab Khan, fell heavily to the ground, and lay there motionless, as if stunned by the violence of his fall.

The Mogul leapt lightly off his horse to inspect, and, if necessary, despatch his fallen foe. The fall and apparent unconsciousness of the robber turned out, however, to be only a ruse. When his own horse was wounded he knew he would be at the mercy of the agile Mogul mounted on horseback, and armed with a bow and arrow that he evidently knew well how to use. It was clear that his only hope was to get his enemy at close quarters, and the best means to effect this object was to fall on the ground and feign death. So when the young Mogul bent over him, the seemingly dead robber's right hand suddenly darted out and clutched his waistband, actually, though he knew it not, grasping the coveted ruby in its place of concealment.

The tables were now turned. The lithe young Mogul was for a moment like a child in the grasp of his burly antagonist, who shook him as a dog shakes a rat. He did not, however, lose his presence of mind, but, seizing his dagger, plunged it again and again into the body of the robber, who was thus compelled to loose his hold in order that he might draw the sword slung at his belt. Mukarrab Khan did likewise. Then commenced in the waning light a duel, in which the superior agility of Mukarrab Khan had to oppose the greater strength of the bandit. Unfortunately for Mukarrab Khan, he could not afford to play a waiting game and wear out his foe till he became exhausted and faint from loss of the blood flowing out of the dagger wounds in his breast. At any moment two or three more of his pursuers might appear on the scene, and he would be overcome by force of numbers. He therefore plied the bandit chief with a ceaseless succession of cuts and thrusts, directed particularly against his unhelmeted head and his unarmed breast.

His adversary, finding great difficulty in parrying the blows, determined to finish the contest by delivering a tremendous stroke at the head of Mukarrab Khan. The descending sword was parried, and in collision with the better-tempered steel of the prince, the robber's blade was shivered to the hilt. While the young Mogul was still staggering under the efforts he had made to ward off this terrible stroke, the robber threw away his useless sword-hilt, and, seizing his battle-axe, advanced once more to the attack, and once more, but with a new and heavier weapon, struck at his opponent with all the strength he had left. Even a Damascus blade could not be expected to sustain the stroke of a heavy battle-axe. So Mukarrab Khan, instead of trying to parry the blow, evaded it by a quick, sidelong movement of his body, and, before the robber could lift the axe again, darted forward and thrust his sword up to the hilt in the heart of his enemy, who fell down dead without a groan.

It was now quite dark, and Mukarrab Khan, after the tremendous exertions he had undergone, was utterly exhausted. He bent his ear down to the ground to listen for the sound of horses' hoofs, and, hearing none, came to the conclusion that the rest of his pursuers had lost the track. So he determined to ride no farther, but to rest for the night where he was. With this intention he whistled for his horse, and, when the docile animal came obedient to his call, led it into a wood by the wayside. There, with the saddle for his pillow, he lay down under a high wall that sheltered him from the cold north wind, and in a few moments was fast asleep.

On the following morning the rising sun shone brightly and the birds were singing their merriest songs in Ghalman, one of the most beautiful valleys of Afghanistan. On either side of the stream which watered the valley there grew abundance of mulberries, apricots, peaches, cherries, walnuts, and poplars. Dost Muhammad, the chief, whose castle crowned the neighbouring hill, derived his wealth not only from the fruit-trees, but also from the river itself, the golden sand of which was caught in thick fleeces spread out under water, and kept in their place by heavy stones. It was spring-time, and the trees were in full blossom, and nowhere was there a promise of a finer fruit harvest than in the garden attached to the chieftain's castle.

In this garden, in the fresh brightness of the early morning, Zuleika, the only daughter of Dost Muhammad, was walking with her two favourite handmaidens. As she walked backwards and forwards she was pleading with the elder of her two attendants to be allowed to open the gate in the garden wall and have a look at the world beyond its precincts. There was, she urged, no likelihood of there being anyone in the wood outside, and she was so tired of the trim alleys of the garden, up and down whose walks she had paced morning and evening as long as she could remember. At last the attendant, after reminding her how angry her father would be if he came to know of it, yielded, and, drawing back the heavy bar, opened the gate. Zuleika immediately stepped forward and stood under the archway, as lovely a picture of grace and beauty as the morning sun ever looked upon. Fearless of being seen by any stranger, her fair brow was open to the fresh morning breeze, that played with the ringlets of her auburn hair. Her eyes, inherited from some Kaffir[1] ancestress, were blue, and her complexion rivalled the rosy tints of the peach-blossoms that grew in the boughs above her head and strewed the green sward at her feet.

Such was the vision that greeted the eyes of Mukarrab Khan as he rose from his hard

[1] The Kaffirs are a fair-skinned race living in Afghanistan, who are supposed to be descended from the soldiers of Alexander the Great.

M 748

"ZULEIKA, ON SEEING HIM, HASTILY THREW HER VEIL OVER HER FACE"

earthen couch on that beautiful spring morning. As Zuleika, on seeing him, hastily threw her veil over her face, he placed his right hand on his breast, and, respectfully bending his head, saluted her with the words "Peace be on you!" in reponse to which she murmured almost inaudibly the customary reply, "On you be peace and the mercy of God and his blessings!" Then, overcome by the shyness natural in a secluded eastern maiden, she retired within the garden.

When she had disappeared, to Mukarrab Khan the sunlight was no longer bright, and the morning hymn of the song-birds sounded harsh and discordant. He had fallen violently in love with the fair girl he had seen for a few moments in the morning sunlight, and how could he, a homeless wanderer, hope to win the hand of the daughter of the rich chief of Ghalman, the towers of whose lofty castle were visible over the garden wall? While such depressing thoughts were passing through his mind, he suddenly remembered the ruby of Hazrat, and when he felt it all safe in his waistband, hope succeeded to despair. This priceless heirloom had descended from father to son through many generations, and had always been kept sacred for a great crisis predestined to threaten the house of Hazrat with extinction. Two hundred years ago a holy prophet, whose predictions never failed, had sung:

> "When the fire of ruin has consumed the garden of Hazrat,
> And of all its beauty only one slender scion survives,
> Then shall the ruby of Hazrat, concealed in the flower of that scion,
> Blaze like the sun, and restore tenfold the beauty of the garden of Hazrat".

The knowledge of this prophecy had prevented Mukarrab Khan's ancestors from tampering with the ruby in any emergency less than that which was indicated in the prophet's verses. Now the conditions of the prediction were fulfilled, and our hero knew that he was justified in using the gem to restore the fallen fortunes of his house. So he mounted his horse and rode boldly up to the castle gate. The chief of Ghalman was an old friend of his family, and sympathized with him in his misfortunes. Nor was he unwilling to give his daughter's hand in marriage to the possessor of the priceless ruby. Without unnecessary delay the marriage was celebrated, for Mukarrab Khan was eager to join the army that the adventurous Babar was mustering for the invasion of Hindostan. In exchange for the ruby his father-in-law gave him five lakhs of rupees out of his well-filled coffers, with which he splendidly equipped a thousand horsemen. At their head he joined the standard of Babar, and fought valiantly by his side on the battle-fields of Panipat and Sikri.

When he returned with honour and glory and his share of the spoils of conquered India, he had no difficulty in overthrowing the neighbouring chieftain who had defeated and killed his brother. Adding the territories of his conquered enemy to his own hereditary dominion, he ruled in Hazrat with more power and splendour than had fallen to the lot of any of his ancestors since the day when the fateful ruby came into the possession of his race. He never repented that the gem had passed out of his hands, as he possessed in its stead what he knew to be a far more valuable jewel, a loving and lovely wife.

The Suitors of Camlavati

THE walled city of Naharghur was situated on the banks of the Chambal, a loop of which encircled half its circumference. The fortified palace of the rajah, a fortress in a fortress, rose high above the river in the middle of the loop. It was defended on the inner side by strong walls against any attack from the city; on the outside the wall of the palace was also the city wall, and the strongest part of the city wall. The part of the palace next to this outer wall was occupied by the zenana, the fair inmates of which enjoyed a wide prospect across the river to the distant mountains that formed the horizon on the west. On a moonless night, an hour or two before dawn, in the month of Jeshtha, four hundred years ago, the beautiful daughter of the rajah happened to look out from her window down to the river-bed below, which was then almost dry. She saw a little spark of light flitting about near the foot of the wall, vaguely wondered what it was, and, without inquiring further into the matter, went off to sleep again. Little did she know that she herself was the occasion of that spark, and that, if she had reported what she had seen to her father, she might have saved him, herself, and the palace from imminent danger.

For the spark was the light of a hubble-bubble[1] passed from lip to lip of the leaders of a powerful band of Mahometan soldiers, who had come with scaling-ladders by forced marches up the river-bed with the intention of surprising the rajah's palace. These bold warriors were animated partly by love of glory, partly by lust for plunder, and partly by iconoclastic zeal, for in the palace was the rich temple of Krishna, with that of his spouse, Rukmini, and their images were known to be adorned with priceless gems and ornaments of massive gold. The young leader, Fath Jang, was fired with the hope of winning for himself a Rajput bride, namely, the rajah's daughter, Camlavati, whose beauty was blazoned abroad over all Rajputana. If he could only win this prize he was ready to give up to his brave followers all the gold and jewels they could

[1] Hubble-bubble=a large pipe, so called because the smoke passes through water and makes a bubbling noise.

seize in the palace of the rajah and in the rich temples attached to it.

The band of warriors had accomplished their long and toilsome march up the river-bed without being discovered. One or two Hindu peasants whom they had encountered on the way they had ruthlessly killed, for fear that an alarm of their approach might be given. They were now taking a few minutes' rest and a hurried smoke and meal to refresh them before they set about the last and hardest part of their perilous undertaking. The bivouac was a weird and not unpicturesque scene. In the indistinct light the groups of bearded warriors in white robes might be seen stretched out in various attitudes of repose on the stony couches afforded by the bed of the river. On one side the overhanging cliff and the high towers of the wall of Naharghur seemed to threaten them with destruction; on the other side rose the black curtain of the opposite river-bank; and above their heads, illuminating with dim lustre the gray pebbles under their feet, shone the heavens, gaily spangled with the radiant stars that shine on the plains and mountains of India. No sound was heard but the gurgle of the hubble-bubble and the murmur of the tiny rivulet tracing its devious course along the river-bed, which in the rainy season was the channel of a mighty river.

Only a few minutes' rest could be allowed. Every moment of delay increased the risk of detection, and might lead to the ruin of the perilous enterprise. Presently Fath Jang, by silently rising from his seat, gave the signal for the commencement of active operations, and his followers, dragging long scaling-ladders with them, climbed the steep bank to the foot of the wall. Silently, without shout or word of exhortation, they applied the scaling-ladders to the wall and began to ascend.

Favoured by the darkness of night, Fath Jang got to the top of the wall unperceived by the inmates of the castle. He immediately leapt down upon the standing ground behind the parapet and attacked the few men who were on guard. He was soon joined by his leading followers, with whose aid he overpowered the sentries. Presently all his 2000 men had climbed the ladders, and the whole body of assailants rushed into the court-yard in the middle of the palace.

Meantime the alarm had been given, and the

sound of loudly-blown war-shells had roused the sleepers. From all the apartments of the palace Rajputs came rushing into the court-yard. The younger and more impetuous had only swords and shields, but older and more experienced warriors soon appeared on the scene in full armour. Then began a sharp fight in the court-yard. The Mahometans, though fewer in number, had the advantage of being arrayed in battle order, while the Rajputs, scattered in isolated groups, could make little impression on the serried ranks of their enemies. Thus the Hindus were soon driven out of the court-yard into the adjacent temples, the durbar-room, and other apartments opening on to the court-yard. One body of the Rajputs that had more coherence than the rest, and was commanded by a leader of commanding stature clad in splendid armour, retired towards the zenana, and occupied the narrow stair leading up to the women's apartments.

The rude Moslem soldiers were for a moment dazzled by the splendid durbar-room, the walls and roofs of which were inlaid with innumerable small mirrors, and gave multiplied reflections of pursuers and pursued. Soon, however, the work of slaughter was renewed and the white marble floors were stained with Rajput blood. Another band of Moslems that broke into the temples of Krishna and Rukmini first slew the priests, and then with the fury of iconoclasts broke all the graven images to be found there. After thus satisfying their craving for blood and their religious feelings, they began to tear from the walls and images the rich ornaments of gold and silver and precious stones that had been offered at the shrines by successive generations of idolatrous worshippers. A third band of Fath Jang's followers that tried to force a passage into the zenana did not fare so well. The defenders of that portion of the palace, under the leadership of the tall Rajput of whom we have already spoken, allowed the Moslems to climb a little way up the staircase, and then rushed down upon them and attacked them with such fury that they were driven out in confusion, leaving two of their number dead on the stone steps.

At this stage of the proceedings Fath Jang's trumpet called his followers to assemble in the middle of the court-yard. According to the plan laid down beforehand, it was now time to slip down the scaling-ladders and retire with the booty they had won. So far everything had gone well with them except the attack upon the zenana. They had wrecked the temples of the hostile gods, and secured a large amount of very valuable and easily portable plunder; but the Rajput bride, on whom Fath Jang had set his heart, was still safe behind the walls of the zenana, the approach to which was guarded by the good swords of twenty Rajputs.

What was to be done under the circumstances? Fath Jang had to decide between the claims of his followers to save their lives by retiring while retreat was still open to them, and his own romantic passion for an alien woman whom he had never seen. Like a good leader, he immediately sacrificed himself for the benefit of his men, and told them to make for the scaling-ladders by which they had ascended.

Unfortunately, when they returned to the wall overhanging the river, they found that some of the fugitive Rajputs had overpowered the men left in charge of the ladders and hurled these down into the bed of the river. Their retreat being thus unexpectedly cut off, nothing was left but to return and defend the palace, which was, at least for the present, in their possession. They were determined, if the worst came to the worst, to sell their lives as dearly as possible.

When they manned the walls they saw from the ramparts that the whole city was rising in arms to drive them out of the palace. A large and well-equipped Rajput army was soon assembled in front of the palace gate. Inside the palace, the only ground still held by the Rajputs was the zenana. Thus the Mahometans were at once besiegers and besieged. They were besieged by the large army outside the walls, and at the same time they besieged the zenana, the entrance of which was still held by the tall warrior and his twenty devoted followers.

Before a missile was discharged from either side, a messenger from the rajah craved admittance to the palace with a view to a parley. On showing his credentials he was taken before Fath Jang and told to deliver his message. He thereupon made a long speech extolling the rajah's prowess and power, and ended by demanding the unconditional surrender of the intruders who had had the temerity to seize his palace. Fath Jang had, however, a trump card in his hand, and was determined to play it with effect. He knew that the Rajputs would never have dreamt of coming to a parley had it not been for the fact that their wives and daughters were at the mercy of the Mahometans. The twenty defenders of the zenana, brave as they were, could not be expected long to maintain their position against a determined attack made by superior numbers of desperate men. This was clearly pointed out to the rajah's emissary by Fath Jang, who not only demanded that he and his followers should be allowed to retire across the border unmolested with their arms in their hands and the green flag of Islam flying above their heads, but also stipulated that the fair daughter of the rajah should be given him as his bride. He also hinted at the possibility and probability of a large Mahometan army, of which his force was an advanced detachment, coming to Naharghur, in which case the city, with its citadel already in the hands of the enemy, would be sure to fall. Fath Jang concluded by suggesting that a single combat might be arranged between himself and any champion whom the Rajputs might select to encounter him. If he were killed or defeated in the encounter he would withdraw his claim to the hand of Camlavati.

With this answer the king's emissary returned. The warlike Rajputs were pleased with the prospect of a single combat. Every distinguished warrior among them hoped that he might have the honour and glory of being chosen as the champion to represent the king and city of Naharghur. But the proposal of yielding Camlavati to be the bride of a Moslem they rejected with scorn. They were willing to risk almost everything else on the fortune of the combat, but would certainly not purchase the honour and safety of the rest of the zenana by condemning the flower of the whole, the rajah's beautiful daughter, to the chance of enduring what they considered a life of degradation and dishonour. As it was evident that they were absolutely fixed on that point, Fath Jang was compelled, however reluctantly, to give it up. After a great deal of negotiation the conditions of the combat were at last fixed. If Fath Jang should win in the combat, he and his followers were to be allowed to leave the territory of Naharghur not only with their arms but also with all the gold, silver, and jewels they had torn from the desecrated shrines. If he lost, the Mahometans were to give up their arms and booty, but their lives were to be spared. Whichever won the victory in the single combat was to carry away as a trophy his defeated adversary's armour.

The terms of combat being settled and ratified by solemn oaths sworn on one side by the Koran[1] and on the other by the sacred water of the Ganges, the rajah held a council of his leading chieftains to determine who should be chosen as his champion to do battle with Fath Jang. Each of the younger chieftains present at the council was convinced that he himself ought to be the chosen warrior, but agreed that, if anyone else was to be selected, Ram Singh, the tall warrior who had defended the zenana so well, would be the best man. So the rajah, when the question was referred to him for his decision, chose Ram Singh as his champion.

The combat was to be fought with sword and shield on a piece of level ground before the gate of the palace. The Mahometans took up their position as spectators in front of the

[1] *Koran*, the Mahometan sacred book.

open gate, while the opposite end of the lists was surrounded by a great crowd consisting of the Hindu inhabitants of Naharghur. In their midst, on a throne facing the gate, sat the rajah, resplendent in cloth of gold, and with rich diamonds and rubies sparkling in the front of his diadem. The ladies of the zenana were accommodated above the gate in a room in the wall, and through screens of carved marble "rained influence" on the combatants, if the eyes of beauty can exert such power when their brightness is thus veiled from the admiring gaze of the young and brave.

An unpleasant incident, that took place just before the champions crossed swords, gave strong evidence of the keen interest one at least of the Hindu ladies took in the combat. Fath Jang, on his way to the lists, happened to turn round to his followers to give them some directions. As he did so, an arrow whizzed from one of the windows of the apartment occupied by the lady spectators, and struck and glanced off the breast-plate which covered his heart. Immediately on seeing this the Mahometans drew their swords, and by loud shouts expressed their indignation at the treacherous attempt. The Hindus, too, at the other end of the lists became wildly excited, and there seemed to be every likelihood of a general battle. Fath Jang, however, allayed the tumult and calmed the angry passions of his followers. He then addressed the assembled crowd in a loud voice. He told them that a missive attached to the arrow showed that it had been shot by Camlavati. No Rajput warrior would, he was convinced, have thus violated the truce so solemnly made. The arrow, he said, had come from the hand of the lady whose beauty had inspired his enterprise, and he accepted it as a symbol of the violence with which the shaft of love had assailed his own heart when he heard by report of the beauty of Camlavati.

After this interruption the two champions advanced into the middle of the lists. Each was a fine specimen of his race, and each recognized in the other a formidable adversary. The Rajput was the taller and more stately of the two. His body, arms, and legs were protected by a suit of chain-mail of elaborate workmanship. The hilt of his sword was a beautiful specimen of ornamental metal-work, in which the artistically-shaped figures were cunningly contrived so as to afford a firmer grasp to the warrior's hand. Even the curved blade was ornamented with figures of animals damascened in gold. His brass shield made in Cashmere was a marvel of embossed work, and was provided with a strong and sharp spike in the middle, so that it was not only defensive, but might on occasion be used as an offensive weapon. As much of Ram Singh's face as could be seen under his plumed helmet showed such regularity of features as is more often seen in Greek statues than in living men and women. His beard, according to the custom of the Western tribes of Rajputs, was divided in two by a short shaven interval in the middle of the chin. Altogether he appeared to be the beau ideal of a Rajput warrior, and it was no wonder that Camlavati looked upon him with more favour than she showed any of her many other suitors.

Fath Jang, in his face, figure, and equipment, was about as different from his Rajput adversary as one strong and valiant warrior can be from another. If his face was wanting in regularity of feature, all its lines expressed energy and decision. His sword and shield and armour were entirely devoid of ornament, but brightly burnished and of the best materials, as had been proved in many a hard fight, the dints of which might still be discerned on helm, buckler, and breastplate. In stature Fath Jang was half a head less than Ram Singh, but he had the advantage in breadth of chest, and his arms were long and sinewy. While the contour of the Rajput's figure under his coat of mail was such as might degenerate into corpulency at a later period of his life, the Moslem was all bone and muscle.

Such were the two men who now advanced to meet in mortal combat. When they came to close quarters the Rajput invited his adversary to deliver the first blow. Whether this invitation was due to a chivalrous generosity or implied an assumption of superiority, it was accepted by Fath Jang, who was a practical soldier, and thought that, when once engaged in combat, he should do his best by all honourable means to kill his enemy. Fath Jang's first blow was delivered with such force that, though half parried, it razed the gay plume of the Rajput's helmet. Then began a rapid exchange of sword cuts, in which the impetuous assaults of the Moslem forced his enemy for the most part to stand on the defensive. The combat seemed very equal. For Ram Singh also was a master of the swordsman's art, and his greater height gave him some advantage. Hard pressed as he was, he showed even in the heat of the combat the courteous chivalry with which he had commenced it. When Fath Jang's foot slipped on a loose stone, he generously lowered his point till his opponent had regained his equilibrium. This action of his was contemplated with different feelings by the spectators. A few nobler spirits applauded his graceful courtesy, while the majority condemned him as a fool for sacrificing any advantage offered by chance in an encounter with such a formidable adversary. Possibly Ram Singh began to take the latter view himself presently, when he began to be worn out by the untiring energy of his opponent, when perspiration began to pour from every limb, and he could not get a moment's breathing space. At last, fearing that he might be defeated through sheer physical exhaustion if the struggle were continued much longer, he determined to make a desperate effort which would probably end the combat. After parrying one of the Mogul's strokes he did not reply with his sword, but gathering himself together under his brass shield and trusting to his superior weight, charged straight against the enemy. So sudden and fierce was his onslaught, that even Fath Jang's sword was not quick enough to strike him as he advanced. The strong spike in the centre of Ram Singh's shield struck the throat of the Mogul and inflicted a grisly wound. The lighter Moslem was borne back two or three feet by the greater weight of the Rajput, and it was with great difficulty that he kept his footing. However, in the end he managed to spring aside, and, as he did so, delivered such a stroke on the helmet of the exhausted Rajput, that he felled him to the ground, where he lay unconscious. Thus in the end Fath Jang stood victorious over his fallen enemy, although the blood trickling from his throat over his breastplate showed how narrowly he had himself escaped overthrow and death.

It is pleasant to record that the terms of the treaty were faithfully observed. Fath Jang and his followers left Naharghur with their arms and the plunder they had seized

M 748

"THE STRONG SPIKE IN THE CENTRE OF RAM SINGH'S SHIELD STRUCK THE THROAT OF THE MOGUL"

when they first entered the palace. Ram Singh, who turned out to have been only stunned and not killed by the stroke of the Mogul sword, soon recovered and married Camlavati.

The Exile

MANY long years ago there was to be seen issuing from the southern gate of one of the great cities of Rajputana a body of soldiers about 1000 strong. There was little of the joy and pride of strength and conscious valour to be seen on their countenances. Though they looked as fine a company of warriors as ever went forth to do battle for freedom and glory, their faces were sad, and they proceeded on their way in a silence unbroken by conversation or song. Saddest of all was their leader, a tall and powerful Rajput prince. The cause of the melancholy that overpowered him and his followers was plainly revealed by his attire. His clothes were black; he bore a black shield and a sword with a black scabbard; and the noble charger that he rode was also black. All showed too plainly that sentence of exile had been solemnly pronounced upon him, and that he was required to leave for ever the land that he loved. His only crime was that he was the eldest son of the great Rajah of Dhir. Although his noble form and character and the valour he had manifested on several hard-fought fields marked him out as in every way well fitted to succeed to the throne, parental partiality for his younger brother, a late-born son, and the influence of a young wife, Sooja Bai, the mother of that younger son, had induced Himmut Singh's father to deny him his birthright and declare his younger brother the heir to the crown. Thus young Bappa Lal, a boy of fifteen, remained in the palace and looked forward impatiently to the day when his old father's death would raise him to the throne, while his elder brother, Himmut Singh, went forth to seek his fortune in foreign lands. He did not, however, go alone, for a thousand of his followers, who had often charged to victory by his side, refused to desert his fallen fortunes. The old rajah was only too glad to let those devoted adherents follow his banished son, so that there might be no one left behind likely to oppose the peaceable succession of Bappa Lal.

However, most of the exiled Rajputs were young, and the high spirits of youth will not long submit to the thraldom of melancholy.

After they had gone some distance and lost sight of the towers and palaces of their native town, their hearts began to revive a little, and many of the more adventurous spirits among them began to look forward, not without pleasurable anticipations, to the prospect of winning for themselves in foreign lands, by their good swords, the position and the glory they were denied at home. After a long march they halted to rest by a stream of pure water in a noble forest, where their bows and arrows soon provided them with plenty of venison for their mid-day meal. They there discussed their plans for the future, which in the sad hours that preceded their departure had been left undetermined. Some were for taking to the hills and raising the standard of revolt in the hope of securing by force their return from exile. This proposal was rejected with scorn by their noble leader. "What!" exclaimed Himmut Singh; "shall we show our love for our country and our desire to be restored to it by lighting up the flames of civil war? Let us rather prove ourselves worthy of our birth by drawing our swords against the enemies of our land and our religion. Are there not plenty of Afghans and Moguls to drive out of

India, that we Rajputs should take pleasure in killing one another?" His spirited words roused the enthusiasm of his hearers, so that they waved their swords in the air and called upon him to lead them to battle, declaring themselves ready to follow him into the very heart of the Mogul Empire.

Accordingly it was arranged that they should make their objective the strong castle of Bar, situated in Mogul territory, about three days' march beyond the Rajput border. As the emperor had lately gone with a large army into Gujarat and drawn most of his forces from the territories bordering on Rajputana, where no serious attack was then to be apprehended, there was good reason to believe that the imperial fortresses in this part of the empire were not strongly garrisoned. If Himmut Singh and his Rajputs by a bold dash across the intervening country could suddenly and unexpectedly appear before the castle of Bar, they would have a fair chance of taking it by a *coup de main.* Once inside the strong walls of that almost impregnable fortress, they might long defy the attacks of the Mogul forces, and might reap a rich harvest of plunder from the surrounding country.

They would almost certainly be all killed by the enemy in the end. But that probability they were prepared to face, provided they could first send at least an equal number of Moslems to the shades below.

So they left the forest with the resolution of men who had made up their mind what to do. After crossing the border, they proceeded southwards by forced marches night and day, making the shortest possible halts. They were favoured by fortune. No Mogul troops were encountered on the way, and on the morning of the third day they saw rising before them the great walls of Bar and the huge rocky hill on which the fortress was built. Here again fortune favoured the brave. Most of the garrison of the castle, fearing no attack, had gone out to take part in a great hunt. The Rajputs, being informed of this, bided their time until the hunting party returned laden with the spoils of the chase. When the gates were thrown open to admit the returning huntsmen, Himmut Singh and his horsemen charged down suddenly from their place of concealment and attacked them, cutting them off from the gates of the castle. Surprised by this sudden onslaught, many of the Moguls were easily cut to pieces, and those who escaped fled into the surrounding country. Those of the garrison who had been left behind in the fortress hurried to the gates and shut them as quickly as possible to keep out the Rajputs. All this had been anticipated by the Rajput leader. He had therefore ordered the main body of his foot-soldiers to go round to the opposite side of the fortress and scale the walls, which, as he expected, were left undefended owing to the rush of the Moguls from the inside to the open gates. The Rajputs climbed like cats up the rock and over the undefended walls. When a sufficient number of them had assembled on the ramparts, they made for the gates, and, quickly overpowering all opposition, opened them wide and admitted Himmut Singh and his horsemen. Thus, with little loss of life, the bold company of exiles found themselves masters of one of the strongest border castles in the Mogul Empire.

The castle of Bar stood on a rocky hill commanding a rich and populous stretch of country. It was strongly fortified on three sides; less so on the fourth, where the natural wall of rock was almost perpendicular, and was much higher than on the other three sides, owing to the action of the river flowing beneath and hollowing a deep bed for itself when swollen by the rains. The Rajputs found the granaries stored with a plentiful supply of grain of different kinds. They also found a number of cattle, which of course were useless to them as food, and only excited their anger against those who could satisfy their appetites at the expense of the holy animal. There was also a fair supply of munitions of war, especially of large stones collected on the tops of the walls, in order that they might be hurled down on any enemy below.

For some time the Rajputs were left unmolested in the citadel they had won. They did not, however, remain inactive, but busily engaged themselves in plundering expeditions against the towns in the neighbourhood, from which they gathered rich spoils. Presently a small Mogul army was sent to check their depredations, and as time went on and reinforcements came in, it became large enough to invest the castle and prevent the Rajputs from venturing into the open. Such siege artillery as was known in those days was brought up, and the blockade was converted into a siege, in which many attacks were made on the walls and repulsed with spirit by the Rajput garrison.

The besiegers soon found that they had no easy task before them. Direct assaults failed owing to the height of the walls and the steepness of the rocks on which the walls were built. Little could be effected by all the artillery that the Mogul governor of the province had been able to get together. The stones hurled by the catapults rebounded harmlessly from the rocky hill, and the two or three old-fashioned cannon brought to bear upon the walls were equally incapable of doing mischief, except one that burst with a loud explosion and caused the death of six gunners.

After that accident, Asaf Khan, the Mogul commander, determined to put his faith in more old-fashioned siege operations. He had several great war-elephants with him, which he resolved to employ as battering-rams to break open the great gate of the fortress. It was, however, impossible to bring the elephants up to the gate under the galling discharges of stones and arrows to which they would be exposed. To meet this difficulty Asaf Khan ordered the construction of a sabat or covered way large enough for an elephant to pass along.

This was, however, easier said than done. The peasants from the surrounding country, impressed to aid in the work of construction, ran away whenever they had a chance of escaping from the whips of the soldiers in charge of them. As most of them were Hindus, co-religionists of the besieged, the task imposed upon them was an odious one, and it was rendered trebly odious by the fact that it was very dangerous and that they were given no pay for their labours. Nevertheless the work proceeded, however slowly. When the sabat had been constructed for some distance, the strong buffalo and cow hides on its roof afforded protection to the workmen bringing materials to the front part, which was still in process of construction. But the nearer the sabat approached the walls, the more dangerous was the position of those building it, exposed as they were to arrows, and even eventually to javelins and stones, hurled at them from the top of the walls. At last, however, after seven or eight days' incessant labour, the mouth of the sabat was as close to the walls as it could be advanced without exposing it to the certainty of being crushed by the huge rock balanced over the gateway, and ready to be precipitated below when occasion required.

On the evening on which the great sabat was completed, a high festival was held in the Mogul camp to celebrate the success achieved. On the following day the battering-elephants were to advance against the doomed gate along the corridor prepared for them. But in this case the besiegers were to learn by bitter experience the truth of the proverb that "there's many a slip 'twixt the cup and the lip". The castle of Bar had originally been a Rajput stronghold. It had an underground passage leading to a sally-port, the existence of which was well known to the Rajput chiefs, and had been carefully concealed from their foes. Himmut Singh, who was as sagacious as he was valiant, wisely determined not to make use of this secret sally-port till he had an opportunity of doing so with crushing effect. He thought that such an opportunity had now come.

On the night of Mogul revelry the sabat

was not as carefully guarded as it should have been. The Moguls had been lulled into a false idea of security against attack by the fact that the garrison had hitherto confined themselves to defending the walls, and had never ventured upon a sally. They did not know that this policy had been followed by Himmut Singh with the express purpose of making the besiegers careless, and that the Rajputs had chafed against the self-restraint imposed upon them by their leader's order. So the besiegers ate, and drank, and made merry, and the sabat was left unguarded except at the end nearest the castle gate.

At about midnight, when the revelry was at its highest pitch, Himmut Singh and 200 of his bravest followers issued silently from the sally-port. Avoiding the front of the sabat, which they knew to be guarded, they poured inflammable oil over the greater part of the construction, and set fire to it at the end farthest from the castle gate. As the wind was blowing from the besiegers' camp towards the castle, the fire, fed with abundant supplies of oil, rushed rapidly in a great mass of flame along the sabat. The labours of many days were thus destroyed almost in a moment. During the sally the besiegers' camp was a scene of the wildest confusion. The Mogul soldiers ran to and fro, uncertain at what point the enemy were to be found. Many of them, being half-armed and carrying torches, presented an easy mark for the arrows and javelins of their foemen, who were shrouded in the darkness of a moonless night. When at last the confusion was somewhat abated and the Mahometans became capable of concerted action, Himmut Singh rang a bell, the sounding of which had been agreed upon as the signal of retreat. As soon as this signal was given, the Rajputs easily disengaged themselves and returned to the sally-port from which they had issued. Besides destroying the sabat, nearly every one of them had killed his man, and, owing to the favourable circumstances and their leader's skill, they had themselves suffered very little loss.

However, the followers of Mahomet are determined men and not easily dispirited. The fact that one sabat had been destroyed was no reason why they should not construct another. Once more the weary work was recommenced.

Having now by a sharp lesson learnt to recognize the daring and enterprise of their foe, they set strong guards to defend the new sabat night and day while it was being constructed. This time, however, the Rajputs made no sally, although they made some vain attempts to set the sabat on fire with combustible missiles. At last the work was once more completed, and the great living battering-rams, or rather battering-elephants, were brought forward for their appointed task.

There were three powerful war-elephants in the besieging army, whose weight and strength were considered to be sufficient to break through the strongest barriers. As the gate of Bar Castle bristled with sharp spikes fixed there with the express purpose of meeting or preventing the impact of the foreheads of elephants, the great beasts were provided with frontlets of thick iron. The howdahs were also made of plates of the same metal, to defend the drivers against the missiles that would be discharged from the wall of the fortress.

One by one the elephants were led along the covered way to the gate. When the first elephant emerged from the mouth of the sabat, it was greeted with a shower of missiles, many of which stuck in its hide. But the driver, who remained unwounded owing to the protection afforded by the iron screen of the howdah, managed to induce the animal to move right up to the gate, which with lowered front it began to batter, reckless of the protruding spikes. Just at this moment destruction fell upon it in the shape of the mass of rock that had long been balanced on the wall just over the gate. The great beast, wounded mortally on the shoulder by the fall of the jagged rock, in its death agony rushed off madly, carrying away with it in its flight a portion of the front of the sabat.

Although this perilously increased the interval of space in which the elephants advancing from the sabat were exposed unprotected to the stones and weapons hurled down by the garrison, it was resolved to repeat the attack immediately, before there was time for another great mass of rock to be poised on the wall above the gate. So the second elephant was driven onwards. Like the first, it sustained without flinching the shower of arrows and spears poured down on it from the walls. But when it was brought right up to the gate and saw the sharp spikes sticking out, it swerved from the encounter, and after a short struggle with its driver fairly turned tail.

The hopes of the Moguls were now centred in the one remaining elephant. If it should fail them, all the labour and blood expended on the construction of the sabat would appear to have been wasted. However, the third elephant showed no inclination to flinch from its task. Unchecked by stone or missile weapon, it advanced resolutely to the attack, and with its armed frontlet levelled the iron spikes on the gates. Then, throwing all its weight into the work, it battered the gate till the timber and iron creaked and groaned again. If Rajputs can tremble, those within the gate, seeing it shake under the force of the elephant's charge, trembled for the safety of the fortress they had so well and so long defended.

But the hour of the fall of the castle had not yet come. Among the heavy stones and sharp weapons with which its hide was assailed, the elephant paid little attention to the slight tickling sensation caused by the end of a rope rubbing against its neck. Yet it was this rope that proved its destruction. For it was firmly fastened to a battlement on the top of the wall, and down it slid Himmut Singh with a sharp dagger in his teeth.

When the bold Rajput alighted on the elephant's howdah, he soon despatched the driver, who had no better weapon to defend himself with than the elephant-goad. The elephant, intent on its battering operations, did not notice what was happening on its back, and continued all the time charging the wall, till Himmut Singh, having killed the driver, crept along its head, and, bending down, hammered a long nail through its skull into its brain with a hammer that he had brought with him for that purpose. As the Rajput bent down and drove in the nail, the wounded animal shook its huge head so violently that he lost his balance and fell to the ground, but not before he had effected his purpose, and rendered the elephant useless for further operations against the castle. Knowing that his end had been secured, he calmly prepared for his death. The Moguls from the sabat rushed out upon him, a hundred against one. But before they could reach him, he suddenly noticed that the rope by which he had descended to the back of the elephant was dangling in reach of his hand. To such an athlete as he was, it was no difficult feat to swarm up the rope. Luckily he escaped unwounded from the arrows shot at him by the besiegers, and soon stood safe and sound among his friends on the top of the castle wall.

After this great failure siege operations began to languish a while. The besiegers set about constructing an artificial mound, which was intended, when completed, to overtop the castle walls. On this work the attention of the opposed forces was now chiefly concentrated. It was probable that the position of affairs would remain unaltered until either the mound was elevated to a sufficient height, or want of provisions starved the garrison into the surrender which their enemies regarded as being sooner or later inevitable.

One evening, however, a startling variety was introduced into the monotonous course of events by the appearance of a local cow-herd in the tent of the Mogul general. This man, though a Hindu, promised for a reward, which would make him by far the richest man in his community, to reveal a path by which access might be obtained to the castle. He admitted that the path was dangerous, as it led up the almost precipitous rock on the north side of the castle. But just on this account the wall was low in that quarter, and if an attacking party once got to the top of the rock, they would have a fair chance of forcing an entrance into the castle. Kasim Khan, a nephew of the Mogul commander, a young and gallant soldier, who had long been hoping for some opportunity of showing his valour, eagerly volunteered to take the lead in the dangerous enterprise.

His request was granted, and in the darkness of midnight, with 500 men specially selected for their courage and agility, he made his way, led by the cow-herd, round the castle to the point from which the perilous ascent had to be made.

At last they crossed the stream that washed the foot of the tremendous precipice, and began to mount it in single file; for, owing to the narrowness of the path, no other course of procedure was possible. The milkman went first, Kasim Khan second, and then his followers, all barefooted and lightly armed. The path went straight upwards in a bee-line, following a course marked by small foot-holes, and occasionally, where the ascent was quite perpendicular, by great iron nails fixed firmly in the rock. Strict silence was observed, and great care was taken to avoid displacing loose stones. Slowly and cautiously the Moguls mounted up and up. When the head of the long line had safely reached the top of the precipice and the foot of the wall, the milkman was pushed aside and Kasim Khan himself took the lead. As has been mentioned above, the wall at this point was very low, and could easily be climbed by a man of ordinary activity. Therefore, now that the rock was scaled, the attacking party had a fair chance of effecting a lodgment in the castle, if only the sentries were absent or could be quickly and quietly overpowered.

With a beating heart Kasim Khan surmounted the parapet, peering into the darkness beyond. Just as he was securing his foothold, a strong arm was suddenly thrust out and gave him a violent push on the breast. The unfortunate young Mogul trembled for a moment in the balance, and then fell backwards right on the head of the soldier who immediately followed him. The two, falling together, involved in their destruction all their followers, most of whom were actually carried away by the impact of their tumbling comrades, while others lost their footing in their vain efforts to get out of the way. The silence of the night was suddenly and horribly broken by the rattling of swords and armour against the hard rock, by the oaths and prayers of the falling Moguls, and by the stones hurled down upon them by the sentries on the wall. One moment Kasim Khan had stood on the top of the battlement full of high hope and battle ardour; the next, he lay a mangled corpse in the water-course a thousand feet below, among the dead and dying followers who had perished under his leadership.

The arm thus opportunely thrust out, which in a moment sent so many Moguls to the other world, was the arm of Himmut Singh. It was his practice at all hours of the night to patrol the ramparts of the castle and see that the sentries were at their posts. On this occasion, as he walked along the northern wall in the deep stillness of that windless night, his keen ear detected the noise caused by a loose stone, which Kasim Khan, as he was climbing up the wall, happened to displace with his foot. He looked over in the nick of time, and, seeing his foeman, pushed him backwards with all the advantage of strength that he derived from his firmer standing-ground.

Meantime the Rajput garrison, in spite of the brilliant success with which it had resisted all secret and open attacks, was so strictly hemmed in that it was impossible for it to obtain any provisions from the country round. The stock of grain in the castle began to be exhausted, and Himmut Singh had to recognize the disagreeable fact that death by starvation was staring him and his followers in the face. Also a letter brought by a trusty messenger came from his wife, telling him that his presence was urgently required at home to save his father from imminent danger, the exact nature of which was not revealed for fear that the letter might be intercepted. On both these grounds he determined to try and extricate himself and his men from a position that could not be much longer tenable.

The night chosen for the attempt proved to be dark and thundery. The Moguls had for a long time been directing all their attention to the construction and defence of the artificial mound in front of the castle. In order that they might be confirmed in their apprehensions of attack in this quarter, a Hindu peasant was bribed to go secretly to the Mogul commander and inform him that Himmut Singh had sworn a solemn oath to level the obnoxious mound to the ground before it rose as high as the castle wall. The success of the attack upon the sabat prevented the Moguls from despising this as an empty threat, and the result was that an undue amount of the besieging forces was continually under arms in the neighbourhood of the threatened mound.

The exit of the Rajput garrison was made on the opposite side, not far from the precipitous rock up which Kasim Khan had led his forlorn hope. Unencumbered by the presence of women and children, they easily and noiselessly descended to the bed of the water-course. Perhaps they might have got clear away without having to strike a blow, had not a flash of lightning suddenly illuminated the scene, and revealed the Rajputs to a group of Mahometan soldiers who were on guard at this portion of the besieging lines. Immediately the alarm was given, and all round the Mogul encampment there was arming in hot haste and hurrying to and fro. Most of the Moguls, however, in accordance with orders given in anticipation of such an emergency as a night attack, concentrated in the direction of the mound, so that there was only a small body of men to bar the path of the Rajputs to freedom and their native land. Their resistance was overpowered after a short struggle, the Rajputs made their way homewards, and on the following morning the Moguls entered the deserted stronghold which had so long defied them.

The Rajputs, retreating northwards by rapid marches, soon crossed the border and found themselves in their own country. Reverently they knelt down and kissed the sacred soil that they had never hoped to stand upon again. At this moment a horseman, riding rapidly southwards, in his haste galloped into their midst almost before he saw them. He attempted to push his way through the encampment and proceed on his way, but his bridle was firmly seized and he was ordered to give an account of himself. He began by telling some fictitious story, but suddenly, seeing Himmut Singh, he gave a shout of joy and surprise and placed a letter in his hand. He turned out to be a messenger from Himmut Singh's wife, bearing a letter written in cypher which conveyed startling intelligence. "Come back at all risks," it said. "Your father is going with Sooja Bai and Bappa Lal to the summer palace. His life or his liberty is in danger."

Himmut Singh on reading this alarming news wasted no time. He congratulated himself on his good-fortune in having met the messenger half-way. But he might still be too late. It was already the merry month of Phalgoon, in which the rajah and his court were wont to go clad in robes of green to hunt in the neighbourhood of the beautiful summer palace, built by his ancestors of marble from the quarries of Mokrano. His father was probably already there, exposed to the intrigues of his ambitious wife and ungrateful son.

Himmut Singh's Rajputs had no horses with them. Although the horse is in the eyes of every true Rajput the object of almost religious reverence, it had been impossible for them to take their beloved chargers with them down the precipitous rocky path by which they had left the castle of Bar. Therefore Himmut Singh had to take the horse of the messenger, and, spurring it in hot haste towards the summer palace, he bade his followers come after him on foot as fast as they could.

A hard ride of five or six hours brought Himmut Singh in sight of the fantastic turrets that crowned his father's favourite summer retreat. He had now to proceed with extreme caution, as he was a banished man, and the discovery of his identity might lead to his death or imprisonment, or at least prevent him from saving his father. He could not show himself openly, and although every moment might be precious, he thought it better to tie his horse to a tree and advance on foot by by-paths through the jungle to the palace. The shades of night, now rapidly falling, made it more easy for him to escape notice. The numerous lights of the palace showed plainly that the court was already there. Himmut Singh, keeping carefully in the shade, approached the walls of the palace, and made his way to a window on the ground floor, from which a most brilliant light shone into the darkness of night.

When he looked through the window, his eyes were riveted on what he saw. His father and Bappa Lal were at their evening meal, the simple dishes of which consisted of venison, pulse, and maize. From the satisfied smile on the old man's countenance he seemed to be enjoying a well-cooked meal, rendered all the more acceptable by a long day spent in the fresh country air. Every now and then he merrily rallied his young son and Sooja Bai, who had superintended the cooking herself, and was now assiduously employing her fan to cool her lord and master and her son, and to keep the persistent fly off their food. The boy seemed ill at ease, and made little response to the good-natured jests of his father. Sooja Bai's brow was adorned with a carcanet of splendid rubies, and pendants of the same precious stone hung from the lobes of her ears. She was dressed in a robe that displayed to the greatest advantage her enchanting beauty. Her sari of mingled gold, purple, and green stripes, wound round her lissome form, made her look in Himmut Singh's eyes like a beautiful baleful serpent, and he no longer wondered at his father's infatuation.

Presently he saw her go to the side of the room to prepare a bowl of sherbet with her own fair hands. There was something furtive in her air which entirely escaped the notice of her doting husband, but not the keen glance of her stepson, who saw that Bappa Lal was also following her motions with stealthy glances. What was that paper that she hastily extracted from a fold in her dress, and the contents of which she poured into the jewelled chalice? In a moment the truth flashed upon Himmut Singh's mind, and without ceremony he burst through the window and stood in the centre of the room.

His father started up in fear and indignation, and clapped his hands to summon his guards from the ante-room. As they rushed in, he called upon them in excited tones to seize the intruder. "Rash young man," he exclaimed, "you shall pay dearly for returning from banishment, and thus violating the sanctity of your father's privacy. You must be either mad or a traitor." "I am neither mad nor a traitor," replied Himmut Singh. "You will find out who is the traitor, if you ask Sooja Bai to make Bappa Lal drink the cup of sherbet she has just now prepared for your honoured lips." On hearing this the fair false face of Sooja Bai became ashy pale, and she fell unconscious on the ground. One of the guards took the cup, and when he had slowly poured out the liquid, there remained sparkling at the bottom a tell-tale little heap of diamond dust, that, but for Himmut Singh's intervention, would have torn the bowels of the Rajah of Dhir, and caused him to die a death of agony.

It was now the old rajah's turn to look pale at the thought of what he had escaped. In a moment his infatuation for his beautiful young wife was changed into loathing, and he recognized the loyalty of his elder son, whom he had so unjustly banished. Bappa Lal and Sooja Bai were kept in strict custody that they might pay the penalty of their treason, and Himmut Singh was restored to favour.

That atonement might be made for the unjust banishment of Himmut Singh in the public manner in which the sentence had been carried out, it was arranged that on the morrow the rajah should return in state to his capital, accompanied by Himmut Singh and his followers, who were not long behind in arriving at the summer palace. The cavalcade was splendid and impressive, and as gay and bright as the retinue which had followed Himmut Singh to banishment just three months before had been sombre and melancholy. Himmut Singh, in a rich robe ornamented with jewels, rode at the right hand of his king and father. His countenance expressed the gladness felt by a patriot when he returns to the native land he had never expected to visit again. Equally joyous were the countenances of the soldiers and citizens, who poured out of the gates to welcome the return of the hero from banishment after glorious conflict with the Mogul foe, and after saving the life of the father who had banished him. The whole city was illuminated that night, and every heart was glad, but gladdest of all was the heart of Himmut Singh's wife when her husband was restored to her.

A Soldier of Fortune

NOT far to the north and south of the border line of the Bombay and Madras Presidencies, and within little more than a hundred miles of each other, lie the ruins of what were once two rich, powerful, and populous cities. They bore the proud names of Bijapur and Vijayanagar, both of which, being interpreted, mean the same thing, namely, the city of victory. Bijapur was a Mahometan, Vijayanagar a Hindu capital, and their ruins at the present day are epitomes of all that is most characteristic of the very different religions and civilizations which they represent. In Bijapur the mosques, now no longer thronged with congregations of the faithful, are beautiful specimens of the skill of the Mahometan architect, who, debarred from embellishing his works with the figures of men and animals, had to devote all his attention to beauty of form, and to such chaste and refined ornamentation as can be produced by the skilfully interwoven tracery of lines. This artistic moderation, more akin to Greek than oriental art, made the mosques fitting temples of the one God to whom Islam bends its forehead in prayer. How different is the wild grandeur bordering on grotesqueness that characterizes the huge temples of Shiva, Krishna, Rama, and the other gods of the Hindu Pantheon, that still rise high from the site of Vijayanagar, although the spaces between are now cultivated fields, from which the peasant with harsh cries frightens the hungry crow!

Three hundred years ago the spectacle presented by Bijapur at a distance was much the same as it presents now to the modern traveller approaching it by the Southern Maratha Railway. A cavalier, well armed and mounted, who in December, 1564, was riding over the ridges to the south-west of the city, saw, much as we may see them now, defined against the horizon, the forms of tombs and mosques and palaces, except that they were not yet dominated by the great dome of the Gol Gumbaz, one of the wonders of the world, which was constructed a century later as a mausoleum for the Sultan Mahmud and his family. He had worshipped in the great mosques at Constantinople, and visited St. Mark's at Venice, and St. Peter's and the Pantheon at Rome; but the great and beautiful buildings that he saw before him, when he entered the gates of Bijapur, were such as could still impress him with wonder after all that he had seen in the most famous cities of Europe. Nor was he less impressed by the crowds of people on foot, in carriages, and on horseback that thronged the streets, all, as he could see, in their gayest attire, as if they were going to some great festival. He enquired of one of the stream of people flowing to the centre of the city what was going on. The man stared with astonishment and said, "Surely you must be a stranger in the country if you do not know that the sultan is holding high festival to celebrate his marriage with Chand Bibi, the peerless daughter of Husain Nizam Shah of Ahmednagar. To-day in the great amphitheatre there are to be combats of animals and bull-fights, and last of all a grand tournament for gallant cavaliers like yourself, the victor in which is to gain as his prize the post of captain of the sultan's body-guard."

Our hero, for such we may call him, thanked his informant, and immediately resolved that he could not better introduce himself to the court and Prince of Bijapur than by taking part in the tournament. If he could win the prize of valour, the captaincy of the body-guard would be a good beginning to his Indian career, and might be the stepping-stone to still higher honours and position. He was a Turk, born in Constantinople, who, after many adventures, had found himself in India, and determined to offer his sword to the Bijapur state, which was at this time continually at war, and might be expected to welcome a good soldier, for such Yusuf Khan certainly was. He was now in the prime of life, and by his valour had won himself a name among the bravest soldiers of Turkey. He had every reason to expect the highest honours that Suleyman the Magnificent so liberally conferred on the defenders of the faith and the empire; but just when one of the principal commands in the Turkish army seemed within his reach, he had the misfortune to be wounded and taken prisoner at sea by a galley belonging to the Knights of St. John. His captors sold him to a Portuguese merchant who was on the point of sailing with a richly-laden argosy for Goa, the great capital of the Portuguese settlements in India. On the voyage Yusuf Khan asked to be allowed to serve among the armed men who had been taken on board for the defence of the vessel and her valuable cargo. Until they came near India the voyage was tedious and uneventful. But soon after they made the coast of India, the ship was attacked at night when she was riding at anchor. In the darkness the pirates came out from their lairs in the creeks of the Malabar coast, surprised the vessel, and clambered on to the deck. They were in such overwhelming numbers that they would certainly have gained possession of the vessel but for the presence of mind of Yusuf Khan, who quickly turned one of the deck guns loaded with grape-shot upon the prow, where the corsairs were clustered in a thick mass. Their numbers only made the discharge more destructive, and before they had a moment's respite from the havoc caused by the grape-shot, Yusuf Khan was in their midst, scimitar in hand, slashing right and left, followed by the bravest of the Portuguese. The pirates were thus either killed or driven into the sea, and the vessel was saved.

The Portuguese merchant was not ungrateful for the good service done to him by his Turkish slave in that hour of peril. When the ship arrived at Goa he immediately gave Yusuf Khan his liberty and a large sum of money, and promised to recommend him for promotion to the viceroy, if he chose to become a Christian and enter the Portuguese service. But Yusuf Khan was a zealous Mahometan, and scorned the idea of giving up his faith for mercenary motives. He thanked the merchant for his kindness, and told him that he preferred to try his fortune at the court of one of the Mahometan kingdoms of the Deccan. The large sum of money received from the merchant he expended on the purchase of a beautiful suit of chain-armour, a pistol, a sword, a shield, and the finest Arab charger he could find in the markets of Goa. On enquiry, he found that there was an immediate prospect of war between Bijapur and the great Hindu kingdom of Vijayanagar. He therefore made no stay at Goa, but immediately went inland in the hope of striking a blow for the Mahometan faith and his own advancement. Thus it was that he found himself, in the end of December, 1564, riding through the streets of Bijapur to the great tournament held in honour of the marriage of the sultan, Ali Adil Shah, and Chand Bibi of Ahmednagar.

When he arrived at the great amphitheatre he told the officials that he intended to compete in the tournament. He was immediately given the hospitable reception due to a stranger knight. They told him that the tournament would not take place till the afternoon, and in the meantime he was assigned an honourable seat not far from the king and his nobles, so that he might have a good view of the opening proceedings. His horse, which fortunately had not carried him far that morning and was still fresh, was attended to in the royal stables, where it was well fed and groomed. Yusuf Khan himself was conducted to an apartment in the newly-built palace called the Gagan Mehel or Hall of Audience, where he could take off his armour and put on for a time the peaceful dress of a spectator. He then took the place assigned to him in the amphitheatre.

Two or three hundred thousand spectators appeared to be thronged on the stone benches, which rose tier above tier all round the arena. Large numbers of those who could not gain admission to the enclosure were collected on the flat tops of the highest of the surrounding houses, or had seated themselves on the branches of the trees that overtopped the wall of the amphitheatre. The show opened with combats between animals, beginning with the gallant little ram and ending with the lordly elephant. The rams butted each other with great spirit, and the sharp clash of the collision of their foreheads resounded all over the amphitheatre. Then two buffalo bulls were pitted against each other. Buffaloes are ugly beasts, not much larger than cows, and when domesticated are gentle enough to be driven by children; but collected in herds in the jungle they are brave and strong enough to tear to shreds any tiger that has the temerity to attack them. The two buffaloes now facing each other in the amphitheatre of Bijapur charged with such fury that one fell like a dead body to the ground, stunned by the force of the impact, and lay there motionless till the water-carriers came up and poured gallons of water over its prostrate form. The next item in the programme was a succession of bull-fights, conducted, not in the cruel and bloody way in which they are managed in Spain, but according to the more merciful and sportsmanlike custom prevalent in southern India. Lively bulls were brought forward with cloths containing sums of money attached to their horns. The bull-fighters were on foot, and their object was to snatch the pieces of cloth from the horns of the bulls. Those who succeeded in doing this were rewarded by receiving the sums of money tied up in the cloths. Thus there was not to be seen the horrible spectacle of gored horses, and bulls cruelly done to death. The only danger was incurred by the men who fought the bulls, and that danger was willingly incurred for the sake of honour and reward. When the bull-fighting was finished, two great elephants were brought forward to do battle against each other. One of them, however, did not relish the possibility of being butchered to make an Indian holiday, and sought safety in flight, to the amusement and indignation of the spectators. The poltroon had to be driven back by means of squibs to meet his adversary, and then the combat between the huge beasts began in earnest. They dashed tusks and foreheads together till they were exhausted by their tremendous efforts, and when they could fight no more were led or driven off to their respective stalls. As soon as the elephants had departed, human combatants took their place in the shape of great Indian and African wrestlers, who strove to overthrow each other in the soft sand. Indian wrestling is a long and tiresome proceeding. A wrestling bout is not decided until one of the competitors lays his opponent flat on his back, and therefore the wrestler who is getting the worst of it throws himself forward prone on the ground, from which position it is almost impossible to dislodge him. By the time all the wrestling matches were finished, Yusuf Khan was beginning to weary of playing the inactive rôle of looker-on, and even the proverbial patience of Indian spectators was somewhat tried.

The next event was a striking and agreeable variety in the proceedings, which delighted the Turkish cavalier as much as the long-protracted wrestling had wearied him. There now appeared on the arena an elephant that had been fed up to the proper pitch of fierceness, and a superbly-mounted officer of the king's body-guard. The officer exasperated the elephant by riding close up to it and waving a flag in its face, and directly the elephant charged, he rode away, on each occasion almost allowing the elephant's tusks to reach the hind quarters of his horse. In order to be able to gallop off with the requisite suddenness, he had to keep his horse, as it were, dancing on its hind-legs when he was near the elephant. Once he tempted fortune too closely, and the elephant's tusks actually struck his horse's flanks. Even in this extremity his fine horsemanship saved him from the destruction that seemed imminent. Though the horse was shaken and almost overthrown by the shock, he kept his seat, and managed to ride off gracefully from his position of peril. The gallant horseman was then summoned to ride up before the throne of the king, who saw where the marks of the elephant's tusks had ruffled the charger's glossy skin. He was presented with a gold chain from his monarch's neck as a reward for his splendid exhibition of horsemanship, and rode away amid the loud plaudits of the spectators.

After this, as it was now nearly mid-day and the sun was powerful, there was an interval of a few hours for rest and refreshment before the commencement of the great competition which was to be the climax of the day's entertainment. Some of the spectators went home, while others remained to retain possession of their seats. Among those who went away was Yusuf Khan. He was too old a soldier to neglect the opportunity of preparing with all due care for the arduous contest before him. So he braced up his muscles by a refreshing Turkish bath, and took a light mid-day meal at the tables provided for strangers by the hospitality of Ali Adil Shah. Then, after a short rest, he armed himself in his armour of proof, and with lance, sword, and shield rode to the amphitheatre, feeling that he would be able to do himself justice in the tournament, and that, if not crossed by adverse fortune, he would have a fair chance of winning the coveted prize. As about fifty competitors appeared in the list, it was arranged that they should first exhibit their skill by tilting at the ring, and that only those who excelled in that exercise should be allowed to engage in the final tournament. To expedite matters, the competitors were required to ride at the ring in parties of four simultaneously. The different parties of four were to tilt at the ring four times each. A considerable number of them managed to bear away the ring three times out of four. Only four were expert enough to succeed at every tilt. Of these four, one was Yusuf Khan; the second was Sidi Hassan, an Abyssinian of great height and breadth, with the muscular development of a Hercules, who held a high post in the Bijapur police; the third was the officer of the body-guard who had already given such a fine display of his horsemanship; and the fourth was a Mogul from the court of the great Emperor Akbar. As these four had distinctly surpassed all the others in tilting at the ring, they alone were granted the privilege of continuing the contest in a more dangerous and more knightly manner. The tournament was to be conducted according to the rules of jousting that were observed in the middle ages, not only in Christendom, but also in Mahometan countries, when Christian and Paynim chivalry

> "Jousted at Aspramont and Montalban,
> Damasco, or Morocco, or Trebisond".

The combat was to be fought *à outrance* with pointed lances, and not with the arms of courtesy. No other weapon but the lance was to be used. Two of Adil Shah's generals were appointed to act as marshals and to decide the award of the palm of victory.

It was determined by lot that Sidi Hassan should first joust against the officer of the king's body-guard. As they took up their positions at the extremities of the lists, all the spectators marked the striking contrast between the burly African and the lithe and supple form of his Indian antagonist. There was a similar contrast between the horses of the two antagonists. The Abyssinian was mounted on a great black charger suited to his heavy weight, while his opponent rode a beautiful bay Arab with a fine muzzle, and slender legs framed rather for speed than strength. When the word was given and they met in full career, the Indian's lance struck Sidi Hassan's shield right in the centre, at the same moment as the point of his opponent's spear glanced off the armour protecting his right shoulder. Such, however, was the difference between the weight of horses and riders, that while the Arab horse was driven back on its haunches and forced to wheel round by the violence of the encounter, Sidi Hassan, on his great black steed, rode straight on unshaken, with no more concern than if he had brushed a fly away from his path. So the marshals had no hesitation in declaring the Abyssinian victorious. Then, after a short interval, Yusuf Khan and the champion from Akbar's court took their positions in the lists, closed their vizors, and met in full career in the centre of the arena. The Mogul's spear went right through Yusuf Khan's shield, and was only stopped in its course by his steel breastplate. Yusuf Khan aimed at the Mogul's head, and hit the helmet over the forehead with such force that he fell stunned on the plain. Yusuf Khan immediately leapt off his horse to give a helping hand to his prostrate adversary, by which act of courtesy he won the good graces of the spectators even more than by the prowess he had displayed. The Mogul soon recovered from the shock so far as to be able to leave the lists leaning on the shoulder of his chivalrous conqueror.

The excitement of the vast concourse of spectators was raised to the highest pitch when Yusuf Khan and Sidi Hassan took their places for the final encounter, which was to close the day's proceedings. The popular sympathy was decidedly in favour of the former, as the Abyssinian had made himself hateful in Bijapur by many acts of tyranny and oppression. Just before the word was given for the charge, the Mogul came forward and offered his own shield to replace that of Yusuf Khan, which his lance had pierced and damaged in the previous encounter. The gift was as gladly accepted as it was generously offered, and this graceful act of gratitude more firmly established the lifelong friendship between the two warriors, the foundation-stone of which had been laid by Yusuf Khan's chivalrous courtesy. All was now ready for the combat. The champions couched their lances, and when the marshals in a loud voice called out *Jane do*—the Hindustani equivalent of *laissez aller*—they met in the centre with a shock that resounded like the discharge of a cannon. The lances of both champions were so well aimed that they were shivered to the hilts. The two horses were driven back on their haunches, and their riders reeled in their saddles. At this crisis the great weight of the Abyssinian, which had added so much to the force of his spear, caused his overthrow. As he swayed on one side, he had to support the whole weight of his great bulk on his left stirrup. The stirrup-leather broke under the tremendous strain, and he could no longer retain his seat, but fell in the dust. Yusuf Khan a second time dismounted from his horse to assist a fallen opponent, but in this case his courtesy was ill requited. He had scarcely reached the ground when Sidi Hassan, whose wild African blood boiled under the humiliation of his unexpected overthrow, sprang up, and, drawing his sword, made a violent attack upon him. Yusuf Khan drew back and defended himself against the furious onslaught, parrying with consummate skill and coolness the tremendous blows aimed in quick succession at his head, body, legs, and arms. The marshals ought to have intervened to stop the gross infraction of the conditions of the tournament which they saw perpetrated before their eyes. But not being prepared for such an emergency, they hesitated, and finally let the combat go on, comforting themselves with the reflection that Allah would defend the right. In the meantime Yusuf Khan had all the advantage that a cool man has over one who is infuriated and blinded by violent passion. For some time he confined himself to defence, waiting to see whether the marshals would come forward and put a stop to the lawless onslaught of his enemy. When, however, he saw that nothing was done, he ceased to retire before his opponent's furious attack, and waited for the opportunity which he knew would soon come. In the meantime even the African's powerful frame was becoming exhausted by the tremendous blows he had been giving under the influence of anger amounting to temporary madness. With a last effort he rushed forward and delivered a great blow at the Turk's head. Yusuf Khan warded off the stroke with the good shield given him by the Mogul, which retained the dint of the blow as long as it continued to be a shield. At the same time, with all his strength he delivered on Sidi Hassan's head a blow which cleft his helmet and broke the thick African skull beneath. Then, and not till then, the marshals came forward and seized the violator of the rules of the tourney. Yusuf Khan's victory was received with loud cheers by the populace, which were redoubled when he was led before the king and presented with a rich robe of honour and a gold-hilted sword.

On the following day Yusuf Khan was formally installed as captain of the body-guard, and took his place at the council held to deliberate on the impending war with Vijayanagar. That great Hindu kingdom was now at its highest pitch of pride, power, and wealth. It was too strong for any one of the Mahometan kingdoms that were its neighbours on the north, and had by recent acquisitions of territory at their expense extended its boundaries to the river Krishna. The Mahometan kings, who had suffered from the power and insolence of Ram Rajah of Vijayanagar, and had themselves swollen his power by their dissensions, were now resolved to unite against the common enemy. The alliance of Bijapur and Ahmednagar was cemented by the marriage of Ali Adil Shah and Chand Bibi. These two powerful states united their forces to make a great effort to crush Ram Rajah and the power of Hinduism. The kings of Golconda and Bedar also entered the confederacy, and led their troops to join the allied army. Religious zealots enlisted in large numbers to take part in the greatest and most promising attempt that had been made to render Islam supreme in Southern India. At least equal numbers were inspired by the hope of getting a share in the plunder of one of the richest cities in the world. In the meantime the proud Hindu king had been arming for the defence of his kingdom, and the Mahometan kings and their principal military officers now met in the palace of Bijapur to consider what would be the best route by which to invade Vijayanagar territory and advance to the attack of the hostile capital.

After a long deliberation, with the details of which we are not concerned, it was resolved that it would be very conducive to the success of the invasion if accurate information could be obtained of the power of the enemy and his intentions. For this purpose a trusty messenger should be sent to Vijayanagar to observe and report what was taking place there. But who was to go on the perilous mission?

"Sidi Hassan would be our man," said the Bijapur general, "but I hear that he has not yet fully recovered from the wound he received in the tournament."

"Even if he were well," said another, "his black skin, thick lips, and gigantic figure are too conspicuous and well-known in Southern India. He would be easily detected, however skilfully he might attempt to disguise himself."

"Let me then go," exclaimed Yusuf Khan;

"I am an entire stranger in the land, and there is little chance of my being recognized. Besides," he added, "I should like to see the great Hindu city in the glory of its idolatrous pride, before the avenging armies of Islam burn its temples and palaces and give its people to the edge of the sword."

After a short consultation Yusuf Khan's offer was accepted, and preparations were immediately made to despatch him on his perilous errand. He thought it best to disguise himself as a Turkish jewel merchant, so that his fair skin and his ignorance of the manners and customs of the people might not excite suspicion. For further protection against detection he put on a false gray beard, which made him look like an old man of sixty. Under his merchant's robe he wore a flexible coat of chain mail. His weapons were a small pistol that he kept concealed for use in emergencies, and a sword which he could wear openly, as in the country through which he had to pass merchants were liable to be attacked by robbers, and were in the habit of going armed. Most merchants, indeed, found it necessary to hire an escort of armed men, but Yusuf Khan preferred to go alone. It would have been difficult for him to engage followers in Bijapur who could be trusted with the secret on the keeping of which everything depended, and the presence of followers who could not be trusted would be a serious addition to the difficulty and danger of his undertaking. The sultan's treasure-house supplied him with a few watches and other curiosities of European manufacture, which were to be represented as specimens of the merchandise he had left in safe custody at Goa.

Thus equipped, Yusuf Khan started on his dangerous errand to the great city of Vijayanagar. Nothing eventful happened on the way. Most of the robbers who infested the debatable land between the two kingdoms had found it more profitable to enlist as soldiers under the banners of the Mahometan or Hindu kings, who were bidding against each other for recruits, than to pursue their trade of plunder. Indeed there were few caravans of merchants to attack, as the immediate prospect of war had brought peaceful commerce to a stand-still. When Yusuf Khan reached the gates of the city, he had no difficulty in gaining admittance. To the very last Vijayanagar gave to foreign merchants of every nation and religion the welcome and protection which laid the foundation of its enormous wealth and commercial prosperity. When the officer of the gate heard that the stranger was a merchant from Constantinople, he immediately gave orders that he should be conducted with honour to the royal palace. Yusuf Khan, following his guide, crossed the river Tungabhadra, which flows along the northern side of the city, by a bridge built of rough granite blocks joined together without mortar, like the structures of Cyclopean architecture in Greece. He then passed along the great Kasbin Bazaar, admiring the solidity of the buildings and the handsome stone arcade on either side, by which the great crowds of buyers and sellers were defended against the heat of the tropical sun. Wherever he turned his eyes he saw great temples and palaces of granite, bearing witness to the wealth of the city and the skill of the architects employed. At the same time, the poor mud huts in which the poorer classes were crowded gave evidence of the great gulf that divided the princes and the rich merchants from the masses of poor toilers who laboured in the quarries, shaped and carried the stones, and by all kinds of manual labour provided their rulers with the materials of their luxury.

After a ride of two or three miles through streets so crowded that rapid progress was impossible, Yusuf Khan found himself before the gate of the king's palace, which, like all the other great buildings of the city, was constructed of great blocks of granite, the rock which not only supplied a great abundance of excellent building material, but also in its unhewn state composed the firm foundation on which the city was built. Through five great gates guarded by soldiers, and through four lesser gates in the charge of porters, he passed into a spacious quadrangle, in which tinkling fountains, shady foliage, and cool arcades of marble combined to vanquish the mid-day heat. Here he was bidden to wait until such time as the king's treasurer should find time to inspect his wares. That proud functionary had nothing particular to engage him at the time, but thought it essential to his dignity to delay a considerable time before summoning the supposed Turkish merchant to his presence. Before sufficient time to satisfy his ideas of what was due to his position had elapsed, he happened himself to be summoned to the king's private apartment. When he arrived in the royal presence, he informed the king that an old gray-bearded merchant from Turkey was waiting below for orders. Ram Rajah, who was deeply interested in all kinds of artistic work, immediately expressed his desire to see what the merchant had brought from distant Europe.

"Have him brought to the reception chamber in the women's apartments," he said, "that I and my beloved Saraswati may inspect his treasures."

The ladies' reception chamber, into which Yusuf Khan was presently ushered, was a marvellous and characteristic production of the skill of the Indian architect and lapidary. The ceiling, supported on white marble pillars, reflected the light from innumerable little mirrors cunningly inserted in plaster, so white and so beautifully chased that it looked like ivory. The walls were inlaid with stones of every hue of the rainbow, so arranged as to represent the history of Rama and the conquest of Ceylon. The king soon came in, accompanied by his favourite wife Saraswati. Four hand-maidens were in attendance with fans in their hands, with which in turns they cooled the brow and cheeks of king and queen. Yusuf Khan immediately made obeisance to the king, whose high rank was revealed by the richness of his robes and the priceless gems that shone in his turban. He was a handsome man in the prime of life. From the features of his finely-chiselled face a physiognomist might have inferred that pride was the predominant element in his character. Not only the king and queen, but also the four women in attendance, showed great interest in the watches and other specimens of European workmanship exhibited by Yusuf Khan. If the supposed merchant was not very clever in explaining the working of the curious toys and the materials of which they were composed, that was set down to his deficient knowledge of the language of the country, and did not excite suspicion.

Now, among the four ladies-in-waiting, one was a fair girl of about fifteen summers, the daughter of a Turkish soldier of fortune, who had come to India with his wife and daughter and entered the service of Husain Nizam Shah of Ahmednagar. He had scarcely been a year in the country when the border fortress entrusted to his care was stormed by the Vijayanagar forces. He was killed in the storm of the fortress, and his wife committed suicide. Their orphan daughter, Ayesha, was taken captive to Vijayanagar, where her beauty gained her admission into the royal zenana as one of the attendants on Queen Saraswati. It was but natural that the sight of the face of a countryman in a strange and distant land should powerfully affect her heart and bring back to her mind tender memories of the Golden Horn, the blue waves of the Bosphorus, and the happy days of her childhood. The terrors that she had undergone, the storming of the fortress commanded by her father, and her residence as a slave in the middle of a hostile and idolatrous city, made India horrible in her eyes. No wonder that when she looked on Yusuf Khan a wild longing seized her to return to her native land. Could not the merchant help her to carry out this the dearest desire of her heart? As these thoughts whirled in quick succession through Ayesha's excited brain, the queen, finding some difficulty in understanding what Yusuf Khan meant, called upon her to act as interpreter.

"You know Turkish," she said. "Ask him how he came to possess that curious intaglio, and what is the lowest price he will take for it."

Accordingly Ayesha went up to Yusuf Khan, and after a few questions and answers in the Turkish language, informed her mistress that the intaglio had come from Italy, that it had belonged to the great Roman Emperor Nero, that the merchant would sell it to no one for less than a lakh of rupees, but that he would feel honoured if he were allowed to present it to the greatest of Indian princes. When the gift had been graciously accepted, Ayesha was again utilized as interpreter, and had other conversations with Yusuf Khan, in the course of which she said to him suddenly and quickly, with a significant look, just before his departure, "Your jewels are valuable, but a brave man might find something still more valuable at midnight before the gates of the great temple." This remark, spoken in Turkish, unintelligible to all except him for whose information it was intended, was supposed to be merely an enquiry about the jewellery. Soon after this Yusuf Khan departed, leaving the intaglio and some of his other jewels purchased by the king, who ordered him to bring all the rest of his merchandise from Goa, as soon as the war was ended, and the mosques of Bijapur and Ahmednagar had been destroyed by the victorious armies of Vijayanagar.

Yusuf Khan, on returning to the room assigned to him in the royal guest-house, could not help thinking again and again over the mysterious words that had been addressed to him. No doubt the impression they produced on his mind was enhanced by the beauty of the girl who had uttered the strange words, and by the glance of a pair of dark, lustrous eyes with which she had emphasized her remark. At any rate he lost no time in enquiring what was the greatest of the Vijayanagar temples, and, learning that Shiva's fane far surpassed all the others in size and grandeur, determined to be there at the hour of midnight, and see whether anything would happen to explain the mystery. The intervening space of time he would devote to making an inspection of the city and taking note of the military preparations.

As he walked through the streets with observant eye, he could see at every turn evidence of the immense efforts that were being made to equip a great army for immediate service in the field. His experienced eye told him that the troops which were being assembled were on the point of taking the field, and that their forward march would not be long delayed. The foot-soldiers were so numerous that it was almost impossible to make an approximate estimate of them. The cavalry seemed to be not much less than 20,000 strong, and the artillery consisted of about 1000 guns. Near the artillery Yusuf Khan saw assembled a great collection of nearly 2000 war-elephants, which he had no difficulty in counting. The din of hammering metal, the blaze of the blacksmiths' forges, and other signs of warlike preparation continued to a late hour of the night; but dead silence prevailed over the great city at the midnight hour when Yusuf Khan made his way to the front of the great temple of Shiva.

He sat down on a granite block and waited anxiously for he knew not what.

No sound disturbed the solemn silence of the night but the ceaseless sough of the wind through the branches of the casuarina tree, the aspen of the East, whose tremulous foliage sighs in the slightest breeze. Everything around him was on a stupendous scale and weighed heavily upon his imagination. Before him rose over the vestibule of the temple, to a height of more than two hundred feet, a great dome in shape between a cone and a pyramid. High up in its walls he could see by the light of the moon slabs of granite thirty feet long, that could, he thought, hardly have been raised to such a height without the aid of demons. Before the entrance knelt the stone figure of a bull, as large as an elephant, carved out of a single mass of granite. A still larger monolithic sculpture was standing near, with the body of a man and the head of a lion. The colossal image was more than twenty cubits high, and over it as a canopy, carved also in stone, spread the hood of a cobra. Wherever he looked on the stone-work and the wood-work of the temple before him the coils of cobras were intertwined in labyrinthine mazes. Even the trees seemed to have been framed by nature in harmony with the temple whose front they shaded, for the tortuous convolutions of the clustered columns of their trunks looked in the misty moonlight like coiling serpents. Add to this that, in the great city surrounding the place at which he sat, lay bound in the bonds of sleep a million Hindoos devoted to the service of countless gods whom he regarded as devils, and it may be realized that Yusuf Khan's mind was almost overpowered by the consciousness of the strange surroundings in which he waited for a sign from the young girl, his countrywoman, whom he had so unexpectedly stumbled upon in the palace of a Hindu king.

He had not long to wait. Hardly had he seated himself, all eye and ear to catch the faintest indication that might be given for his further guidance, when from the shade of a neighbouring clump of sacred bael-trees he heard sung in the faintest tones a few notes of a Turkish national song. In the same low voice he took up the refrain and walked over to the clump of trees. There he found waiting for him, thickly veiled, the young Turkish girl whom he had seen in attendance on the queen. She was so overpowered with shame at her audacity in seeking an interview with a stranger at such an hour, that for some time she could not speak. At last she found her voice, and said softly, with her face bent to the ground:

"Ah! my friend and countryman, what will you think of me, shameless as I am, for having sought this interview? But what could I do? Think what a life I have lived for the last twelve months, shut up among idolaters and strangers in the palace of an accursed king, who is guilty of the death of my father and mother. If, considering all this, you still condemn me for venturing out to seek counsel of one who is not only a Moslem but also speaks the dear language of my native land, kill me at once. Real death would be far better than the living death I endure. If, however, you can pardon my shamelessness, tell me whether you can help me to escape from this terrible place, if not to my native land, at least to Bijapur or some other country in India where true believers rule or where Allah is worshipped."

"Sister," replied Yusuf Khan gently, "no just person would condemn your action. What would be immodest conduct on the part of a girl living in a happy Mahometan home under her parents' care is praiseworthy in your unhappy case, condemned as you are to be the bond-slave of infidels. It is not pleasing in the eyes of Allah that any true believer should willingly submit to the yoke oi idolaters."

"Then help, oh help me," she prayed, "to escape from this city, which is surely doomed to destruction for its idolatry and pride."

Yusuf Khan paused for a moment in deep thought, and then said:

"Lady, stranger as you are, I place my life in your hands. Know that I am no merchant, but a soldier. I have been sent here by the

King of Bijapur to find out the strength of the Vijayanagar army, and the military plans of the king and his generals. If I am discovered, death is certain. If I escape with such information as I can collect, I may do a great service to the Mahometan kings who are now advancing to attack this great stronghold of Hinduism. By to-morrow night I hope to have gained all the information in my reach. On the next morning I leave Vijayanagar. If you can again find means to escape from the palace, disguise yourself as a page-boy, and meet me on that day a mile beyond the stone bridge over the Tungabhadra. If you can do this, I promise to devote my good sword to your service like a true knight, and either conduct you safe to Bijapur or die in your defence."

"I will spend my last jewel in bribing the door-keeper to let me out once again," she replied. "And now, farewell till we meet again on the road to Bijapur."

She was turning to depart when she paused and said, "But have I not any information to give you on the warlike matters which must interest you more than the fate of a poor, weak girl? I have overheard whispered conversations between the king and queen, in which he boasted of the plans he had formed for the overthrow of the Mahometan armies. Have you not in your army an Abyssinian called Sidi—Sidi—I forget the other name?"

"Hassan," eagerly replied Yusuf Khan. "What of him?"

"Yes, Sidi Hassan. That was the name. Well, he is a traitor, and has promised to lead the army of Bijapur into an ambush at the ford of Ingulgi, where a thousand cannon will be concealed, ready to pour their fire on the Mahometan troops as they pass."

"Lady," said Yusuf Khan, "this is indeed priceless information, which, if we ever get safe to Bijapur, will gain you great honour at the court of the queen. Can you remember anything more of what Ram Rajah said to his queen?"

"I can remember nothing more," she said, "but the king's boasting and unholy joy at the thought of the destruction of the true believers. And now again farewell, or I shall be missed, and then—"

So saying, she swiftly disappeared.

When Yusuf Khan returned to the guest-house he was seized by the chief of the Vijayanagar police and carried off to prison. The king had shown his treasurer the purchased jewels, and the treasurer remembered to have seen one of them in the palace of Bijapur. On hearing this, Ram Rajah immediately divined the true object of Yusuf Khan's visit to Vijayanagar. He called the chief of the police and said to him:

"Go immediately and cut off the head of the Turk who has come to the guest-house. Or no; on second thoughts, shut him up in safety, and when we return victorious from Bijapur we will have him and thousands more of the accursed Mahometans trampled under the feet of our elephants."

So Yusuf Khan was put in prison, and informed that he would not get out till the king's elephants had returned from the war, and were ready to trample him and other captive Moslems to death.

We must now change the scene to the banks of the river Krishna, where more than two hundred thousand troops were assembled ten days after Yusuf Khan had been thrown into prison. On the south of the ford of Ingulgi was the great army of Ram Rajah, at a sufficient distance from the river to render it invisible from the northern bank, towards which the Mahometan armies were advancing in battle array. The Vijayanagar artillery, cunningly concealed from view, was arranged in two long lines on the east and west of the ford. All the cannon were loaded, so as to be ready at a moment's notice, when the signal was given, to pour a tremendous cross-fire on the hostile troops as they crossed the ford and struggled up the southern bank of the river. The troops of the Mahometan kings were marching on, apparently unconscious of danger. By his own request the duty of scouting had been entrusted to the traitorous Abyssinian, who had ridden across the ford and returned, reporting that no enemy was to be seen. He now led the van of the Bijapur army, and it had been arranged between him and Ram Rajah that, when he had decoyed the whole advance guard, forty thousand strong, across the river, he should suddenly give the spur to his horse, and gallop over the intervening space to the front rank of the

Hindu army. His doing so was to be the signal for a thousand cannon to pour shot and shell on the doomed Mahometan advance guard, which would, it was hoped, be utterly destroyed before it could be reinforced from the northern bank of the Krishna.

Sidi Hassan on his black charger rode in front of the whole Bijapur army, accompanied by Yusuf Khan's Mogul friend, who had volunteered to serve in the campaign, and had asked and received a post of honour in the vanguard. They had almost reached the river when they became aware of a horseman coming from the east and urging his weary horse to the utmost exertion by voice and spur. He had good reason to do so, for it was Yusuf Khan, escaped from his prison in Vijayanagar, and he knew that the fate of thousands of Mahometans depended on his being in time. The Abyssinian was for moving on without further delay into the ford, but the Mogul, who was riding by his side, implored him to wait the arrival of the horseman, who might, he said, be the bearer of important tidings. While this discussion was going on, Yusuf Khan came near, and was recognized.

"Thanks be to Allah," he exclaimed, "that I am in time!"

He then turned to Sidi Hassan, whose hand sought the hilt of his sword as he called on the troops under his command to advance to the ford.

"Dog of an Abyssinian," he cried out in a loud voice, "order an immediate retirement, or you will die the death of a traitor on the spot."

"And who are you," replied Sidi Hassan, "to give orders to me, and incite my followers to mutiny?"

So saying, he drew his sword and rushed upon Yusuf Khan, hoping to slay him before he could divulge his double-dyed treachery. But the Turk was too quick for him. He drew a loaded pistol from his bosom, and, as Sidi Hassan raised his sword to strike, shot him dead through the heart.

It might then have fared ill with Yusuf Khan but for the protection of his Mogul friend. The Bijapur troops, not understanding what had happened, and only knowing that their leader had been slain, closed round him with threatening gestures, and were inclined to take a life for a life. The Mogul, however, appeased them by taking Yusuf Khan's sword and pistol, which he willingly surrendered, and assuring them that he would be conducted to the presence of Ali Adil Shah and required to account for his conduct. So Yusuf Khan was taken before the king, and told the story of all that had befallen him on his perilous expedition. Ayesha had been at first reduced to the lowest depths of despair when she heard in the palace the news of Yusuf Khan's arrest. However, she immediately determined to leave no stone unturned to procure his release. He had scarcely spent a week in prison when, by the promise of a large bribe, she induced one of the jailers, who was a Mahometan, although, being in the service of a Hindu king, he concealed his faith, not only to let him go free, but also to restore him his sword and pistol and provide him with a good horse. Yusuf Khan's escape from prison and from Vijayanagar was rendered more easy by the state of anarchy to which the city had been reduced by the absence of the king and all his forces. He had, however, to make a long circuit in order to avoid the danger of being captured by the widely-extended Vijayanagar forces. Thus it was that he arrived at the ford of Ingulgi only just in time to save the Mahometan vanguard from destruction. He had hardly finished his story when its truth was confirmed by the Vijayanagar army, which now began to show itself by thousands and tens of thousands on the opposite bank. Ram Rajah had been informed of the death of the Abyssinian by his scouts, who were concealed in the reeds of the river-bed. So, seeing that the great scheme of ambush had failed, he ordered his artillery to advance and cannonade the enemy across the river. Additional confirmation of the Abyssinian's treachery was found when his body was examined, and letters of instructions from Vijayanagar were unrolled from the inmost recesses of his turban. So he was left unburied by the banks of the Krishna, a rich feast for the vultures, who were already following the track of the contending armies. The command of the Vijayanagar vanguard, left vacant by his treachery and death, was conferred on Yusuf Khan.

The cannonade of the Vijayanagar artillery inflicted little damage on the Mahometans, who retired from the river and took up a strong position farther back. A council of war was then held to determine the future plan of the campaign. It was clear that the great Vijayanagar army was strongly entrenched for the defence of the ford of Ingulgi, and that any attempt to force the passage there would be madness as long as the numerous and powerful Hindu artillery commanded the ford. It was therefore resolved to entice the Hindu army from its strong position by marching slowly along the northern bank of the river towards the ford of Dhanur, which was ten miles higher up the stream. It is matter of history that the device succeeded. The Vijayanagar forces kept pace with the enemy along the opposite side of the river, and presently entrenched themselves on the southern bank of the Krishna at the ford of Dhanur, as strongly as they had before entrenched themselves at Ingulgi. Then the Mahometans in the darkness of night suddenly doubled back to Ingugli, crossed the ford there without opposition, and drew out their armies in order of battle on the southern bank.

Ram Rajah, having been thus outgeneralled, had to give battle to the enemy on equal terms to save his capital from attack. Then began, on the morning of January 25th, 1565, what is known in Indian history as the battle of Talikoti. It was one of the greatest and most decisive battles ever fought on the soil of India, and ended in a triumph for the arms of Islam in the East, which almost counterbalanced the loss of the battle of Lepanto, six years later, in the West. The battle of Talikoti was for a long time evenly contested. For a while the Mahometans were dismayed by the thousands of rockets discharged in the air by the enemy's artillery. Their wings were thrown into disorder by brilliant charges of Hindu cavalry. But their centre, the van of which was commanded by Yusuf Khan, pressed on slowly and irresistibly in serried ranks against the Vijayanagar centre, where Ram Rajah in person could be seen directing the operations of his troops, conspicuous to friend and foe, on his great war-elephant. Against him Yusuf Khan directed the attacks

M 728

"THEIR WINGS WERE THROWN INTO DISORDER BY BRILLIANT CHARGES OF HINDU CAVALRY"

of the Moslem van. He knew that the fall or capture of the mighty king would do much to decide the day, and he was animated by personal feelings of revenge, remembering how he had lain in prison for seven days and nights waiting for the time when he would, in accordance with the king's orders, be trampled to death by elephants. Again and again the bravest of the Hindu troops came forward in succession to interpose between the king's elephant and the advancing enemy, but still Yusuf Khan moved on relentlessly, always making the king's elephant the object of his attack. At last Ram Rajah's heart failed him. He did not know of the success of his cavalry on the two wings, and quailed before the continual attacks directed against his sacred person. So he slipped down from his elephant, and got into his state litter, which was close at hand. But the bearers were terrified, and refused to perform their office. So he mounted on a horse from which a devoted follower dismounted. In the meantime the Hindu warriors in the centre, no longer seeing their king, and fearing he was slain, began to waver and give way. The confusion was increased by the 3000 or 4000 war-elephants belonging to either side, which went raging about the field of battle, and, as was their wont, did as much harm to friend as to foe. But through all this confusion Yusuf Khan did not lose sight of his quarry. He was not far from the royal elephant when the king dismounted. He saw him creep into his litter, and then followed close on his heels when he mounted on horseback. In the close-packed crowd of fugitives rapid flight was impossible. Yusuf Khan soon caught him up, and with one sweep of his sword severed his head from his body. The fallen head was picked up by a Moslem soldier, who fixed it on a long spear, and, holding it aloft, displayed it to both armies. The sight of their great king's head fixed on a spear completed the discomfiture of the Hindu army, which fled in headlong rout from the battle-field, mercilessly pursued by their enemies.

After the utter rout of their great army and the death of the king under whose auspices they had so often been victorious, the citizens of Vijayanagar could offer little resistance to the armies of the four Mahometan kings. The great city was captured and sacked, and its temples for the first time had to submit to the blows dealt by the iconoclastic zeal of the victorious Mahometans. Yusuf Khan did not forget the fair girl to whom he owed so much. His first care was to protect the palace and those therein from outrage by proceeding there with the king's body-guard, whose devotion to his service he had secured by his valour. When he returned to Bijapur, so great was the glory he had won that he might have married a princess of the royal blood. But love and gratitude were more powerful in his mind than the ambition of being connected by marriage with the Sultans of Bijapur. He married the beautiful Ayesha, who had saved him from prison and from the prospect of a cruel death. After his marriage he continued to serve with distinction in the Bijapur army, of which in the course of a few years he became the commander-in-chief. But neither he nor his wife forgot their native country. They did not wait for the approach of old age in India, but after ten or twelve years' residence in Bijapur returned with their children to Turkey. So at last Ayesha realized the seemingly hopeless dreams that had solaced the misery of her captive state, and once more saw the domes and minarets of her beloved Stamboul.

The Lost Casket

SHIVAJI and his followers, after their raid on Surat, had retired loaded with plunder to their fastnesses in the south. We of the English factory had successfully defended our lives and our property, thanks especially to the valour and discretion of our president, Sir George Oxenden, and to the guns and sailors he summoned to help us from the ships at Swally. But my uncle was terribly distressed. He had lost what he valued almost more than his life, a small casket containing a beautiful miniature of his dead wife set in rubies and diamonds, and also the *Agnus Dei* which the Martyr King had presented to him twenty years before for his devoted loyalty in the great rebellion. The casket containing these and other precious relics had been forgotten and left behind in my uncle's villa when we hurriedly retired from it to take refuge in the factory. The villa had been thoroughly ransacked by the Mahratta spoilers. On our return we found little remaining but the bare walls, and the casket was nowhere to be seen. No doubt it had gone with the rest of the plunder of Surat to Shivaji's new capital on Raighur, and there was little hope of its ever being recovered to gladden once more my uncle's eyes and heart.

My uncle as a stubborn Malignant (such was the cant term the Roundheads applied to anyone conspicuous for loyalty to Church and King) had been deprived of his landed estates in England by the rebel government. With a little money saved from the wreck of his fortune he started life again as an India merchant in Holland, and had thriven so well that he was now extremely rich. In the last of several voyages that he made to India he took with him me, his nephew, the penniless orphan of his brother, who had fallen on the fatal field of Naseby. Although I had done my best and won my rich relative's approval, I did not take very kindly to a mercantile life. Indeed, I felt far more in my element when assisting in the defence of the factory against Shivaji's marauders than when engaged in the purchase of the embroidered stuffs of Ahmedabad, Broach, and Cambay. The excitement of the street fighting roused in my heart the latent spirit of adventure that had descended to me from a long line of warlike ancestors, and I became more discontented than ever with the prosaic routine of a merchant's office.

In this state of mind what seemed a happy thought suggested itself. Why not make an expedition into the Mahratta country and try to recover the lost casket? Its contents were of no intrinsic value, and I could safely promise a large number of rupees in my uncle's name if they were given up. No doubt the adventure was a dangerous one, and might almost be called foolhardy. But the element of danger was a positive attraction to one who had been for two or three months repining at the dull monotony of mercantile life. There was also another motive urging me on. Before leaving England I had fallen sorely in love with the fair daughter of the lady in the miniature. Although my poverty and dependent position prevented me from declaring my passion, a lovely rose bestowed on me at parting gave me reason to hope. It seemed to me that nothing would be so likely to make my uncle look favourably on my suit as the recovery of the casket that contained the symbols of the strongest feelings of his heart —his reverence for his murdered king and his love for his long-lost wife. But why analyse the motives that urge a young man to hasty action? On the impulse of the moment I determined to go, and I went.

It was not, however, advisable to inform my uncle of the project. In spite of his longing for the lost relics, his gray-bearded wisdom would certainly have forbidden my departure. So I made my arrangements secretly, and took no one into my confidence but a Soorti groom called Gopal, whose courage and good faith had been proved more than once. I supplied myself and him with the best weapons procurable. He was armed with a sword and a dagger. I also had a sword girt to my side, and in addition a pair of pistols in my holsters. We were mounted on country-bred horses, not very beautiful to look at, but capable of enduring much fatigue, and able to climb up mountain-paths that would infallibly have broken the legs of an English hunter or charger.

Thus mounted and accoutred, we started soon after sunset in the end of January. I shall never forget the beauty of the scene that greeted us as we began our journey. Before us the planet Jupiter shone in the eastern sky; behind us Venus was suspended just over the houses of Surat; and above us in mid-heaven the half-moon "threw her silver mantle" (I quote from the verses of a crop-eared poet who ought to be hanged, drawn, and quartered as a regicide, but whose poetry may challenge comparison with the noblest works of Greece and Rome) over the plain and gave enough light to keep our feet from stumbling. In the daytime at this season of the year the earth is dry and brown after three months of unbroken sunshine, but at night, under the magic of the moon, all looks as bright and fresh and beautiful as fairyland. As we rode on through the cool of the night, my spirits, under the excitement of adventure, rose so high that it was impossible for me to refrain from singing aloud. In the morning, when we had put some thirty miles between us and Surat, we sent a messenger back to inform my uncle where we were going and with what object, in case he should think that his nephew had been kidnapped.

It is not necessary to give the details of our long and rapid ride from Surat to Raighur. We were often threatened, but never seriously molested on the road. Now and then groups of bandits hovered near us, as if they would attack us. On such occasions I would hand one pistol to Gopal and hold the other in my own hand ready for action. The natural result was that the marauders held aloof scowling. They saw that little was to be expected from us but hard knocks, and preferred to wait for an easier prey. When the waning moon failed us, we bivouacked at night and started in the cool, crisp air of the early morning, which gave us keen appetites. In spite of Mahratta raids, the country through which we passed was not deserted by the country people, as Shivaji never allowed his followers to plunder the poor agriculturists. Unfortunately we could get nothing from them to eat but chupatties[1], milk, and fruit.

[1] Chupatties = Indian cakes resembling Scotch scones.

Even eggs were rare luxuries, and sometimes the villagers proved churlish, and would give us nothing to eat for love or money. So we often had to ride long distances with our belts tightened round our empty stomachs in a manner far from agreeable to a healthy Englishman. But for this serious drawback our ride on the track of Shivaji was a pleasant journey. There was much of interest to note in the manners and customs of the strange people of the country. The mountain scenery of the Ghats towering on our left hand was grand and imposing, but the description of such matters may be left to more practised pens. I have a plain, unvarnished tale to tell, and must hurry on to the great object of the journey, our visit to Shivaji.

At the town of Mhar we overtook the last of the train of bullock-carts that were conveying to Raighur the plunder of Surat. They were guarded by an escort of twenty-five troopers under the command of a havildar[1]. As soon as they saw us, they closed round us in a menacing semicircle, while we stood on our defence with our pistols loaded. The

[1] Havildar = petty military officer.

Mahratta horsemen formed a picturesque group. They were armed with sword and shield and spear, and clad in frocks of quilted cotton, capable of offering considerable resistance to a sword-cut. Most of them had gold or silver ear-rings attached to the backs of their ears, and their thick moustachios gave them a look of valour and ferocity. Their leader in a loud voice ordered us to give up our arms. This we refused to do. A parley ensued. I asked what they proposed to do with us if we gave up our arms. The havildar replied that he would take us before the maharaja[1], who was at Raighur. I replied that this was what we wished, but that we would not surrender our arms until we reached the royal fortress. Let them therefore choose whether they would take us as we were, or forcibly disarm us at the risk of their lives. The havildar consulted with his men. They had no firearms, and it was evident that the pistols in our hands were likely to kill two men if we were assailed. So they came to the conclusion that discretion in this case was the better part of valour. As we were willing to

[1] Maharaja = great king. Shivaji was the Mahratta maharaja.

go to Raighur, it would be foolish to risk their lives for a mere punctilio. So, on receiving my solemn promise that we would surrender our arms at the gate of Raighur Fort, they took us on with them in their company and treated us in the most friendly manner for the rest of the journey.

A stiff climb brought us up to the first gate of Raighur. Here, according to our agreement, we gave up our swords and pistols to the captain of the gate. Within the walls of the fortress we had little to fear from random violence, and if Shivaji chose to put us to death or imprison us, our weapons would be useless. As we struggled up the steep and narrow pathway by which alone the hill-top is accessible, and saw above us the frowning bastions commanding the approaches to the gates, we marvelled whether such a stronghold could ever be captured except by the aid of famine and treachery.

After we had passed through the third and last gate we were conducted before the killedar or commander of the fort, who, on hearing that I wished to see the rajah, assigned us quarters for the day, and informed us that we should probably be permitted to attend the Royal durbar[1] on the morrow. After we had rested and refreshed ourselves with curry and rice, and cool draughts of water from a spring in the rock, we strolled round the fort, which was held by a garrison of 2000 or 3000 men. The number of private and public buildings was about 300. Except on the side by which we had ascended, the mountain was girt with tremendous precipices which required no artificial fortifications. In our walk round the fort we were accompanied by a Brahmin clerk, who explained all the arrangements and the purpose of everything we saw, and was never tired of extolling the wisdom and valour and greatness of his king. We were also followed by a small company of soldiers, nominally as an escort, but really intended to prevent us from carrying out our evil intentions if we contemplated doing any mischief.

As the afternoon shadows began to lengthen, our guide told us that he might be able to give us a glimpse of the rajah. We were full of curiosity to see the man of blood. We had heard of the assassination of Afzul Khan by

[1] Durbar = reception.

his own hand, and of the still more treacherous assassination of the Rajah of Jowlee, a Hindu like himself, whom he had done to death by the agency of others. My friend Mr. Smith, captured by the Mahrattas at Surat, had told us how ruthlessly Shivaji had ordered the cutting off of the heads and hands of those brought before him. I therefore pictured him in my imagination as a man with the face of a devil, surrounded by fierce followers with drawn swords ready to execute his cruel mandates and defend him against the just rage of his oppressed subjects. The real Shivaji pointed out to us by our Brahmin guide was very different from the creature of our imagination. He was seated on a stone bench by a well, with no escort near him, and was talking pleasantly with the women who came to draw water, and asking them kindly about their husbands and brothers. The children at the well came up to him fearlessly with smiling faces, and he was giving them fruit and sweets that he had brought with him for the purpose. As, ourselves unseen, we scanned his features from our point of observation, we said to ourselves that we had never seen a face more expressive of kindness and more attractive. Whatever he might be to the foes of his nation and his religion, he was evidently the father of his people, and deserved their affection as fully as he had earned the fear and execration of their enemies. This new view of his character was abundantly confirmed during the rest of our stay at Raighur. Every Mawali and Hetkuri with whom we conversed spoke about him in terms expressive of mingled love and veneration as the saviour of the Mahratta nation and the pillar of the Hindu religion.

My next sight of Shivaji was on the following day at the great durbar, when the spoils of Surat were spread out to gladden the eyes of the rajah and his principal followers. The plundered treasures of Surat made a fine show. The principal jewels were spread out on a large and costly Persian carpet. There were strings of pearls, great diamonds, rubies, and emeralds, some unset and some set in jewels of heavy gold, and I saw among the rest my uncle's lost casket. About twenty or twenty-five lakhs of rupees in silver and gold money had also been extracted from the unfortunate city, but these were by this time safely lodged in the treasury. Shivaji himself was, of course, the central figure, seated on the *gadi*[1], and wearing a red turban surmounted by a beautiful diamond aigrette. This time I was able to observe his features more closely than when he was seated by the well. Unlike his followers, he grew a beard after the manner of the Rajputs, from whom he claimed descent. His form was slight and supple, and rather less than the middle height. His long arms gave him great advantage as a swordsman. His skin was fair for an Indian. His nose was long, and curved like the beak of a parrot. He had a bright and restless eye, full of intelligence, and whenever he made any remark to those around him, he accompanied his words with a pleasant smile. On a lower and smaller cushion sprawled his dearly-loved son and heir, Sambhaji, then a boy of seven years, and doomed in the future to live an evil life and die an evil death, distinguished by none of his father's good qualities but personal courage. Close behind Shivaji stood Moro Punt Pingley, his peishwa, and Tannaji Malusray, the bravest of the brave, his comrade in the killing of

[1] Gadi = royal cushion or throne.

Afzul Khan, the attack on Shaisteh Khan at Poona, and other deeds of blood and valour. Right and left of the *gadi* there were suspended on gilded lances emblems of power and sovereignty, among which I noticed gold heads of fishes with large teeth, and horses' tails, and high above the rest a pair of gold scales, equally balanced to represent the even-handed justice of the rajah.

It was not easy to get admission to the durbar, and it promised to be a still more difficult matter to gain the favour of a private interview with Shivaji. The Brahmin clerk, who was our informant on all subjects, told me that, according to the immemorial customs of the East, those who sought audience of a prince must first make handsome presents to his ministers. It was therefore incumbent on me to consider what I could present to Shivaji's chief advisers, especially to Moro Punt Pingley, the peishwa. I replied that I had absolutely nothing with me worthy of their acceptance except my pistols, which I proposed to offer to the rajah himself. This difficulty, which at first seemed insuperable, was suddenly dissipated by the rajah's curiosity to see me.

After a delay of a day or two he himself sent for the English stranger, and I was accordingly admitted to the royal presence.

After making my obeisance, I was asked the motive that had led me to visit Raighur. I replied that I had come in the first place that I might see the person and capital of a great king, who was threatening to overshadow the glory of the Great Mogul, and in the second place that I might petition for the restoration of a casket of little intrinsic value, but very dear to its owner, which was to be found among the spoils of Surat. On being asked what return I proposed to make for such an exceptional favour, I was fairly gravelled for a reply. Not having the face to offer a great king two or three hundred rupees, as if he were a shopkeeper, I could only contrive to make some rather lame remarks about the beauty of disinterested benevolence, and how an act like this would, in the words of Shakespeare, become a monarch better than his crown and sceptre. The monarch before me did not, however, seem to be much moved by the sentiment borrowed from Shakespeare. In the pleasantest manner possible he replied that the plunder of Surat was the property of the state, and that he would be sacrificing the interests of his people if he gave up a single pie[1] of it for nothing or for mere sentimental reasons, especially for the benefit of any member of a nation which had obstinately opposed the operations of his troops at Surat, and shown no disposition to submit to his authority. He added, however, that he had no wish to quarrel with the English, as he had lately shown by letting his captive, Mr. Smith, go free, instead of yielding to the wish of his followers, who had been most anxious to cut his head off. He had no wish to harm me either, and would give me a safe-conduct back to Surat, and I should think myself lucky in escaping so easily from the lion's den into which I had so rashly entered. Nothing more could be said. After I had left the royal presence, I was informed that I must leave the fort within three days and return by ship to Bombay or Surat. In case the rajah should relent, I thought it advisable to remain at Raighur for the three days granted us, although weary of the rice and pulse boiled

[1] Pie, a very small Indian coin worth about a twelfth of a penny.

in butter apportioned to us as our daily fare, and longing to return to the flesh-pots of Surat.

We were allowed considerable freedom in going about the fort and seeing all that was to be seen. On the evening after my interview with Shivaji, I went with the Brahmin clerk to a lonely part of the mountain which commanded a wide prospect of the surrounding country. On an overhanging eminence we stood gazing at the view long after the sun had sunk behind the hills on the west. When the increasing darkness warned us to return, we suddenly found that we were not alone. A single Mahratta soldier was moving slowly, as if absorbed in deep thought, across our path. Immediately afterwards we saw that he was being stalked by three other men, who followed him step by step, crouching cat-like under the shadows of trees and rocks, and so intent on their quarry that they did not notice us. All of a sudden, when they were a few yards from us, they threw off all disguise and concealment, and with naked swords rushed upon the solitary figure before them. The object of their attack, with remarkable agility threw off his fit of abstraction and the heavy shawl in which he was wrapped, and, drawing his long sword, ran swiftly to a narrow passage between two rocks, in which his three assailants would not derive so much advantage from their numerical superiority. Here he stood at bay. I hurried to his assistance, though armed with no more formidable weapon than a stout bamboo walking-stick. With this, however, I struck a heavy blow just under the ear of the hindmost of the three assassins, and felled him to the ground. This was their first intimation that they had more than one adversary to deal with. The unexpected rear attack entirely disconcerted them. The man next to the one whom I had stunned turned savagely on me, and thrust his sword under my arm. He plunged it in up to the hilt, luckily not in my heart, but in my thick overcoat. Before he could disengage his weapon I closed with him, and, exerting all my strength, for he was a strong man, threw him on his back on the ground. The only way to keep him there was to jump on him and sit on his stomach, which I accordingly did. Seated on this heaving air-cushion, in spite of its struggles to shake me off, I was able to watch the progress of the encounter between the two remaining combatants.

What was my surprise to discover that the man whom I had so opportunely assisted in a terrible danger was the great Mahratta king! He seemed to be in his element when engaged at sword point with a foeman worthy of his steel. His enemy was a taller and stronger man than himself, but Shivaji more than made up for these disadvantages by the quickness of his movements, and his wonderful dexterity in the use of his weapon. His sword, Bhowani, flashed here and there with the rapidity of lightning. The other was so busy parrying the ceaseless succession of his thrusts, that for a long time he had no opportunity of delivering a counter-stroke. When at last, in despair, he ventured to do so, Shivaji, instead of parrying the blow with his sword, evaded it by a quick backward turn on his right heel, and at the same moment drove Bhowani through the heart of his enemy, who fell dead at his feet.

When the great king, after the combat, came towards me, I involuntarily half rose to do him obeisance. The man beneath me immediately took advantage of this slight movement, and by a desperate effort succeeded in shaking me off. Uttering a wild imprecation against Shivaji, he rushed away straight over the brow of the precipice, and I saw him no more. He could not possibly have got safe to the bottom, and must assuredly have fed the vultures on the rocky slopes of Raighur. After following the fugitive with his eyes till he disappeared from our view, Shivaji turned to me with a winning smile and said:

"Brave Englishman, you have to-day saved my life, and thereby averted a great danger from my nation and my religion. Let us for the moment forget the differences of race and creed and shake hands in your frank English fashion. To-morrow come and see me again and ask whatever you will, for there is nothing I can refuse to one who has done so much as you have done to-day for Maharasthra."

So we shook hands as men do who have proved each other in time of peril, and then proceeded to inspect the man whom I smote under the ear with my bamboo stick. To our surprise he was quite dead. At this moment the Brahmin clerk, who had promptly run off for assistance, came hurrying up with a body of soldiers. All stood in amazement when they saw the two dead bodies, and Shivaji with his reeking sword. The latter simply told them, "Three men attacked us in the dark. One, by the help of the gods and my good sword, I slew. The second fell under the blows of this brave stranger, whose walking-staff is like the club of Bhima. The third fled." Nothing remained to be done that evening but carry off the dead bodies.

The assassins turned out to be Mahometans, who had thought to gain the joys of Paradise by killing the great adversary of Islam in India, or perishing in the attempt.

On my way to the audience chamber next morning I met with reverential salaams[1] and friendly smiles on faces which before had regarded me with looks of sullen suspicion or contemptuous indifference. Everywhere clear signs of popular favour were manifested.

[1] Salaam (peace), oriental greeting.

Some of the Mahrattas even went the length of procuring me a dish of butcher-meat. The stewed kid (they never roast meat in this country) was very acceptable after such a long restriction to vegetable diet. It is needless to say that there was now no difficulty about the return of my uncle's casket. The great prince graciously received my pistols, which I presented to him as being, however unworthy of his greatness, an appropriate gift for a famous warrior like himself. He was pleased to admire their workmanship, and to reply that no more fitting gift could pass from one warrior to another. He placed round my neck a necklace of priceless pearls, and bade me ask for whatever my soul desired. Remembering what Dr. Broughton had won for his countrymen under somewhat similar circumstances at the court of Shah Jehan, I made bold to ask for the granting of trading privileges to the English in the rajah's dominions. He replied that he was quite willing to admit English merchants and manufactures into his country, and that, if an embassy came to Raighur on the subject, he would give it a hearty welcome.

On the following day, loaded with rich presents, I descended with my trusty Surti groom to Nagotna, whence we sailed for Surat in one of the best ships of Shivaji's navy. My uncle gave me a hearty welcome back, though he reproached me for the rashness of my conduct. "Foolish boy," he said, "the dearest wish of my heart has long been that you should marry my daughter. As I now know from your rash expedition and her letters that you are neither of you inclined to oppose my wishes, we shall return to England in a month or two and light the marriage torch." And so the pearl necklace of Shivaji adorned on her wedding-day the white neck of the fairest maid in England.

THE END

NOTES

Page

9. **gallant**, handsome and brave looking.

Mogul. The name given by the Hindus to the rulers of the House of *Baber*, which under *Akbar* became paramount in India.

Rajputana, the land of the Rajputs, a Hindu race which claims descent from the ancient Kshatriya or warrior caste, and which is the ruling race, though not the most numerous in the country.

Akbar. The great Mahometan sovereign (1542–1605) who practically founded the Mogul Empire.

Gujarat, a part of India which includes the northern districts of Bombay, the Gaikwar's dominions, and several other native states.

spick-and-span, perfectly new and fresh.

accoutrements, military dress and arms.

10. **troopers**, horse soldiers.

anticipated, looked forward hopefully to.

converging, coming on to a place from another direction, drawing nearer to.

cavalcade, procession consisting chiefly of people on horseback.

immured, shut up in.

zenana, the part of the house in which the women are confined.

closely-veiled, having curtains all round.

shielded her from the eyes, &c., kept the people who passed from seeing her.

11. **their progress was interrupted**, they were stopped.

pounced, leapt out suddenly.

Page

the fair occupant, the pretty girl who was inside the litter.

lap of luxury, in the habitual use regardless of expense of what was choice and costly,

tender mercies of bandits, cruelties and brutalities of robbers. An example of the figure of speech known as *oxymoron* (sharp dull), where by means of seemingly contradictory terms an idea is emphasized.

pleading gaze, look of entreaty, look begging pity.

sheer terror, utter fear.

trembling fingers refused, &c., her fear was so great that she had no power in her fingers, and was unable to unfasten the pearls, &c.

12. **a picture of misery**. She looked so wretched and unhappy that she might have been taken for the symbol of unhappiness.

rakshasas, demons.

love at first sight. He fell in love with her the moment he saw her. Compare "Whoever loved who loved not at first sight". (*Marlowe*.)

13. **taking advantage, &c.**, meanly getting what he wished because the girl was unable to hinder him from doing so.

honour won the day, he decided to do what he thought right.

however sore, &c., no matter what his grief was.

14. **endure heavy penance**, be punished severely.

obliterate the image, &c., make her forget the young man who saved her.

Page

dinted, bore the marks of, had hollows in them from.

javelin, a light spear thrown from the hand at a foe.

15. **had enjoyed his fill**, had had enough of fighting to satisfy him.

proved his manhood, shown his bravery.

honour and glory, the distinction and praise.

dissipate or mitigate, disperse or make him feel less keenly.

melancholy reigned, &c. He was very sad and sorrowful.

burning ghat, where Hindus burn their dead.

16. **funereal white**. White was worn as a sign of mourning for the dead.

bier, carriage on which dead body was borne.

jowari, a course kind of millet.

sati, the burning of a widow along with the body of her dead husband. The word really means a faithful wife.

17. **heart and soul**, whole-heartedly, enthusiastically.

imperial edict, &c., that the decree of the emperor was obeyed.

immolate, offer herself in sacrifice.

prevented her. Among Hindus widows were not allowed to remarry.

18. **evil omen**, a sign of ill luck.

object of loathing and contempt, a thing greatly disliked and scorned.

refuse to survive, say that she would not live after.

rake out, pick out with care from the ashes of the pyre.

impassive, without feeling.

19. **tumultuously**, in great swelling waves.

she had developed, &c., she had grown from a pretty girl into a lovely woman.

grasped the situation, understood what he saw meant.

untimely, while still quite young, before your time.

20. **baulked of their prey**, seeing their victim saved, snatched from their hands.

Page

taken into account, thought of any value.

ghouls, demons or evil spirits supposed to prey on human bodies.

21. **crupper**, the part of the horse's back behind the saddle.

the burning ground, the place where the bodies were to be burned.

bar the progress, &c., prevent Abbas Khan and Tulsibai going forward.

close quarters, within reach.

delivered, &c., struck a blow that made the opponent senseless.

charged straight, rode full speed right at.

22. **shrank from**, &c., did not try to go on with the fight.

induced to acquiesce in, led to permit or allow.

evil choice, choice of evils. Note the figure of speech employed. It is called *hypallage*.

lead, &c., did as Akbar himself had done.

23. **Padishah**, king.

prime of life, he had not begun to fail or grow old.

patronage, the help and encouragement he gave.

pinnace, a kind of rowing boat usually with eight oars.

Houris, nymphs or maidens of the Paradise of Islam. The name is sometimes applied to any exceedingly lovely woman.

rose and the bulbul, the rose and the nightingale. The bulbul is a kind of thrush much admired in the East for its song, and is therefore often called the nightingale of the East. It is represented as in love with the rose.

24. **Sita**, the wife of Rama, the hero of the Indian epic the *Ramayana*, was carried off by Rawana, king of Ceylon. Rama invaded Ceylon and recovered Sita. These adventures and the subsequent return to Oudh as king, his banishment of Sita, his reunion with her, and his translation to heaven, are the subjects of the epic.

what accursed unbeliever, &c.? to what idolatrous Hindu, condemned for her unbelief in God

Page

and his prophet Mahomet, was she married?

celebrate, make my song in praise of.

paint her, say she is, describe her words.

confirmed the poetic panegyric, &c., showed that the poet's praises of her beauty and her attainments were generally thought correct.

25. **amorous**, inclined to love.

signify, give intimation.

destined, intended by fate.

harem, the part of the house of a Mahometan reserved for the women of the family.

stainless pedigree, all his forefathers had been high-caste Rajputs.

feigned compliance, pretended he was willing to let his daughter marry the Padishah.

suzerain, overlord, feudal superior.

contemplated insult, the proposed adding to the Padishah's harem of a daughter of his.

according to circumstances, as things turned out.

26. **gorgeously caparisoned**, splendidly equipped or fitted out.

reception, the carrying back when handed over.

barbarian, semi-savage.

wusunt, bridal present.

presumes to woo, &c., has the impudence to ask for his wife.

war to the knife, pitiless war till one or other was beaten.

precipitancy, haste.

27. **to conciliate**, to win the favour or gain the good opinion of.

ramparts, outer fortifications or defences, the parapets.

rungs, steps of ladders.

was foiled, was rendered useless.

rigorous investment, complete cutting off of the place from communication with the outside world.

28. **terms of capitulation**, conditions on which it would be allowed to yield.

Page

pollution, soiling, defiling, degrading of their families.

averted, prevented.

immolating, sacrificing.

base sentiments, unworthy thoughts.

exposed them to opprobrium, made them subjects for blame and abuse.

martial harness, outfit for war, armour and offensive weapons.

29. **raised at night**, built up during the night.

Rajputni, Rajput woman.

with all due ceremony, with every care that all the prescribed forms were observed.

saligram (*salgram*), a black stone found in the river *Gandak*, and thought a symbol of Vishnu.

Apsaras, female divinities produced from the sea, and living in the sky as the wives of the Gandharwas, the singers at the feasts of the gods.

who would never meet again, who were going to death.

30. **death agony of their race**, the whole tribe was sacrificing itself determined not to live dishonoured.

the umbrella is looked on in many parts of Asia as a symbol of royalty.

precedence, order, which should go first.

swarga, the heaven of Indra and of the lesser gods.

first onset, beginning of the assault.

31. **rallying centre**, where the soldiers from all parts of the field could gather together.

considerable time, a long time.

animating, &c., encouraging, heartening them for the attack.

the scene of action, where the battle was being fought.

consummated Rajput vengeance, put the finishing touch to Rajput's punishment for wrong.

girths, bands round belly of elephant holding on howdah.

32. **tide of battle became stationary**, neither side was able to drive

Page

the other back, or seemingly to gain any advantage.

superior numbers, &c., there were many more Mahometans than Rajputs.

muscles were become exhausted, their arms were tired with their efforts.

33. **they coveted**, they desired strongly for themselves.

umbrella of state, the umbrella was among the Rajputs a sign of kingship.

34. **Din**, faith; the party cry of Mahometans in quarrels with those of other faiths.

depressed in spirits, sad, gloomy, downcast, in low spirits.

holocaust, great sacrifice of life. lit. burnt-offering.

35. **degenerate girl**, girl who had lost the noble qualities of the race to which she belonged.

36. **amnesty**, a general pardon for past offences.

auspicious occasion, event which promised better things for the future.

at the summit of his wishes, having gained all he most wished to gain.

37. **swollen with pride**, was filled with thoughts of his own greatness.

at the summit of prosperity, seem to have gained everything worth gaining.

38. **obnoxious to the power, &c.**, most hateful to the gods, who by their power will cast them down from their prosperity.

smile of love, &c., smile that showed how fond he was of the girl, and how sure he was that he could guard and guide her.

reduced to the level, &c., acted just like an ordinary man.

envenomed cloth, cloth that had been made poisonous.

39. **gruesome**, making one shudder.

with mingled feelings, glad in some ways and grieved in others.

41. **the extensive ramparts**, the defences which were of great extent, and therefore needed many men to hold them.

Page

alternatives, two things one of which must be chosen.

scanty forces, &c., small number of men they had for the defence.

to obtain relief, to get help.

42. **stared them in the face**, seemed to them the only things that could happen.

suffer such an indignity, endure such an insult.

protracting negotiations, &c., lengthening out the bargaining about terms.

eagerly expectant, anxiously waiting for the final decision.

43. **brightened his declining years**, made his old age happy.

playfulness and affection, fondness for fun and love of others.

could elicit a reply, could drag an answer from him.

death warrant, document authorizing the execution.

44. **sybil**, a woman who foretells what is to happen.

characteristic, what those who knew Punna would have expected.

45. **Bhil**, an aboriginal race of northern Central India.

fleshed his maiden sword, fought his first fight.

'the course of true love never did run smooth.' It means that before they can wed true lovers have always great difficulties to overcome. The quotation is from Shakespeare's *Midsummer-Night's Dream*.

46. **cherishing in her heart, &c.**, thinking often and fondly of the young soldier.

her ideal of manly beauty, &c., she could think of no one better looking or braver than he; nor did she think it possible that there could be such a one.

Rakhi, Hindi form of raksha, a bracelet.

47. **picture of hopeless dejection**, looked downcast as if he thought things would never be better.

subject of controversy, a thing to be debated about and quarrelled over.

49. **mollify him**, put him in a good temper again.

Page

60. **conveying it, taking the ring.**

leaguer, besieging army.

tortuous, winding.

51. **the most critical**, the most difficult or dangerous.

finding his struggles useless, discovering that he could not get away, however hard he tried.

pretended, &c., made a show of ceasing to try to get away.

53. **retraced his steps**, walked back.

rather an encumbrance, &c., more in the way than it was useful.

54. **discovered him to the eyes, &c.**, let the besiegers see him.

in hot haste, very quickly.

55. **diminishing in number**, growing fewer and fewer.

signs of exhaustion, marks of being tired out.

56. **in accordance with his request**, as he begged to be.

57. **generous resolution**, kindly or noble purpose or intention.

turned traitor, been false to his side.

58. **forlorn hope**, the body of soldiers chosen to begin the attack on a fortress.

obstruct these operations, hinder those things from being done.

feint, unreal, pretended.

pressed home, pushed on to the end, the gaining of their object.

59. **a practicable breach**, an opening in the defences through which it would be possible for the besiegers to force their way.

effected, made.

cut the communications, get between them and where they drew their supplies from.

60. **established themselves**, encamped and made the necessary arrangements.

61. **superior mobility**, ability to go from one place to another with greater ease and speed than the forces opposed to them.

deprived of his artillery, having had his guns taken from him.

operating in his rear, making attacks on his forces from behind, and preventing supplies, &c., coming up.

62. **beginning to run short**, to give out, the supply of food was now being seen to be not enough.

63. **bastion**, the fortification projecting from rampart and commanding foot of wall on each side.

the beleaguered garrison, the soldiers in the fortress.

64. **had to be abandoned**, had to be stopped, given up.

inflict a decisive defeat on, beat utterly, completely.

66. **excited by their success**, carried away by the harm they had done the enemy.

extricate itself, draw itself free or clear.

fetched a compass, made a circuitous, or roundabout journey.

68. **concentrate**, to gather together at a particular place.

greeted as their deliverer, welcomed as their saviour.

69. **meed**, reward.

all the fruits of victory, all the benefits expected to be got from beating the enemy.

scene of action, where the fight was going on.

70. **unmolested on its retreat**, free from attack on its way back home.

chivalry, &c., kindness, courtesy, and bravery.

71. **regal tiara**, royal crown.

72. **Fragrant blossoms strewed, &c.**, sweet-smelling flowers were scattered on the road along which they went.

73. **glades**, the grassy pathways through a forest.

Aravalli, the name of the mountain range running from south-west to north-east across Rajputana or Rajasthan.

74. **quarry**, the game he was chasing.

75. **opportunely**, in good time.

Diana, the huntress goddess. She was considered by the Latins to be the same as the Greek goddess Artemis, the sister of Apollo, and one of the great Greek deities.

Page

These were supposed to have their abode on Mount Olympus.

as transitory, &c., passed very quickly and was very pleasing.

76. **creatures of his imagination,** things he had fancied to exist, not real things.

77. **attained wonderful skill, &c.,** became a splendid shot.

rakshasa, demon, evil spirit.

78. **somewhat declined, &c.,** past his prime, growing old.

83. **proved fatal to the whole enterprise,** made the undertaking fail.

admirable promptitude, &c., splendid quickness to grasp what should be done.

84. **was foiled, &c.,** found himself unable to shut the gate.

performed prodigies, &c., did many wonderfully brave deeds

retrieve the fortunes, &c., to snatch victory out of the seeming defeat.

85. **as bulwarks, &c.,** as strong defenders of the freedom of the Rajputs.

87. **stood aghast, &c.,** looked with shrinking and horror.

mullah (mulla'), a learned Mussulman, the mosque officer who calls to prayers, and usually leads them.

fallen into an ambush, been led into a trap.

89. **suspected of treachery,** thought that he had gone over to the enemy.

at a moment's notice, as soon as the order was given.

90. **a gorilla,** the largest, strongest, and fiercest of the apes.

92. **Babar,** a grandson of Timur's great-grandson, and the founder of the Mogul Empire in India.

93. **spurned by a hundred hoofs,** kicked out of the way as of no consequence and ridden over.

conspicuous, standing out clearly from the others.

swiftness he had to restrain, he was forced to hold in the horse, not let it go as quickly as it could have gone.

94. **free from the constraint, &c.,** no longer held back, allowed his head.

nobly responded, &c., quickened his pace to the utmost of his power when urged by his rider to do so.

baser competitors, &c., less noble or speedy strugglers in the race.

wearied and hopeless, tired out and knowing their efforts were useless.

95. **recklessly cast away,** threw off and dropped without counting the cost.

96. **stunned, &c.,** made unconscious by.

only a ruse, merely a trick to cheat.

burly antagonist, big and strong, and somewhat rough opponent.

97. **waning light,** light growing less and less.

superior agility, greater powers of moving rapidly.

his pursuers, the robber's followers who had been unable to keep up.

directed particularly, &c., aimed especially at.

was shivered to the hilt, was broken to bits.

98. **trying to parry, &c.,** to receive the stroke on the blade of his sword.

tremendous exertions, &c., very great efforts he had made.

utterly exhausted, thoroughly worn out.

docile, well taught.

99. **crowned the neighbouring hill,** was built on the top of the hill close at hand.

golden sand, sand mixed with gold. The heavier gold sank to the bottom, and so was caught in the fleeces.

100. **beyond its precincts,** outside the wall.

trim alleys, the carefully-kept pathways.

Fearless of being seen, she did not think it possible that there could be any stranger to see her.

Page

Kafir ancestress, Kafir woman from whom she was descended.

greeted the eyes, met the look.

101. **secluded Eastern maiden,** Eastern girl confined to the harem, and not permitted as European girls are to meet people freely.

to win the hand of, to be allowed to marry.

heirloom, a piece of personal property which has long been in possession of a family.

102. **predestined to threaten,** that must by fate's decree happen to.

whose predictions never failed, what he foretold always happened.

one slender scion, one slim young member of the family.

indicated in the poet's verse, spoken of or described in the poem.

103. **for the invasion of Hindostan.** Babar defeated Ibrahim Lodi at Panipat, 1526.

in overthrowing, in beating in battle.

104. **Chambal,** Central Indian river.

encircled half its circumference, went half-way round it.

enjoyed a wide prospect, had a very extensive view.

Jeshtha (*Jyeshth* or *Ieth*), the month corresponding nearly to June.

105. **imminent danger,** a misfortune threatening to befall a person or thing.

love of glory, wish to gain fame.

iconoclastic zeal, desire to destroy images held sacred.

blazoned abroad, &c., had been pictured in glowing terms all over the land.

106. **bivouac,** an encampment in the open air without tents.

gaily spangled, dotted over brightly.

107. **devious course,** winding course.

the risk of detection, the danger of being found out.

perilous enterprise, dangerous thing they had set out to do.

108. **arrayed in battle order,** drawn up as they should be when fighting.

Page

serried ranks, lines drawn closely together, in close touch.

110. **everything had gone well,** they had won everywhere.

easily portable plunder, captured stuff that could easily be carried.

romantic passion, &c., his fancied love for a woman of another race.

111. **to sell their lives,** to kill as many of the enemy as they could before dying.

devoted followers, men ready to die for their leader.

unconditional surrender, yielding without receiving any promises as to how they would be treated.

temerity to seize, daring or impudence to capture.

112. **stipulated, &c.,** laid it down as a condition.

113. **prospect of a single combat,** the chance that there would be a battle between a chosen fighter on each side.

conditions of the combat, the place, time, and way the battle should be fought.

114. **settled and ratified,** fixed and agreed to by both parties.

115. **accommodated above the gate, &c.,** were placed in a room over the gate.

rained influence, &c., made each of the fighters more and more determined to do his best.

expressed their indignation, gave utterance to their surprise and disgust.

116. **allayed the tumult,** put a stop to the excitement and disorder.

interruption, break in the proceedings.

formidable adversary, an enemy not easily to be beaten.

beautiful specimen, &c., a fine example of the effect the artist in metal can produce.

117. **damascened in gold,** worked in the blade in gold after the fashion of Damascus blades.

embossed, shaped by being raised above the general surface.

Page

defensive weapon, one used for protection against attack.

offensive weapon, a weapon used in attacking.

energy and decision, vigour and firmness.

118. **devoid of ornament**, without any decoration.

had the advantage, &c., was broader.

degenerate into corpulency, &c., grow fat as he grew old.

119. **stand on the defensive**, be content with guarding himself.

till his opponent, till Fath Jang was again firm on his feet, and prepared to go on with the fight.

condemned him as a fool, thought him silly for not taking advantage when his enemy slipped.

sacrificing any advantage, not making use of any favourable incident.

120. **how narrowly he had escaped**, how nearly he had been beaten.

the terms of the treaty, &c., the bargain entered into was kept.

122. **proceeded on their way**, marched on.

melancholy that overpowered him, lack of spirit, gloom that had the mastery over him and made him unfit to do anything.

revealed by his attire, shown by his dress.

123. **valour he had manifested**, bravery he had shown.

on several hard-fought fields, in several fiercely-fought battles.

devoted adherents, faithful followers.

thraldom of melancholy, submission or yielding to gloom or hopelessness.

124. **hearts began to revive a little**, they began to regain their spirits, ceased to despair.

their bows and arrows soon provided them, they were able with their bows and arrows to shoot.

had been left undetermined, had not been fixed.

Page

Afghans and Moguls, successive invaders of India.

125. **make their objective, &c.**, try to capture.

were not strongly garrisoned, were not held by large bodies of men.

coup de main, a sudden and strong attack which carries the enemy's position.

almost impregnable, could only be taken with very great difficulty.

126. **send to the shades**, kill.

favoured by fortune, had good luck.

returned laden with, came back carrying with them the animals they had killed.

127. **had been anticipated, &c.**, the Rajput leader had guessed what would be done.

overpowering all opposition, beating all those who tried to hinder them.

commanding, overlooking and controlling.

128. **swollen by the rains**, made much larger than usual by the rains.

useless to them as food. The Hindus do not eat cow's flesh.

satisfy their appetites, &c., appease their hunger by eating the flesh of the cow.

in plundering expeditions, &c., in journeys and raids in search of what things of value or use they could take by force.

check their depredations, put an end to their plunderings.

invest the castle, lay siege to the fortress.

129. **Little could be effected**, no great injury could be done to the Rajputs.

battering-ram, a large beam with a head of iron, so hung that it could be used for breaking down the walls of a fortress.

130. **co-religionists of the besieged**, people who believed generally the same things about God and duty that the holders of the fortress believed.

in process of construction, in the way of being made or built

Page

131. **a high festival**, a great feast of rejoicing.

to celebrate, &c., to mark their joy at what had been done.

"there's many a slip", &c., that often the things we most certainly expect do not happen and we miss the good things of which we felt sure.

sally-port, a place through which the garrison can make an attack on the besiegers.

132. **confined themselves, &c.**, done nothing more than try to defend the walls.

ventured on a sally, dared to come out and attack the besiegers.

revelry was at its highest, &c., the rejoicing and the fun were at their height.

133. **the confusion was somewhat abated**, there was less disorder.

easily disengaged themselves, separated themselves without difficulty from those with whom they had been fighting.

134. **their appointed task**, the particular work set for each to do.

135. **it was greeted, &c.**, clouds of arrows, spears, bolts, and stones were hurled against it by the garrison.

destruction fell upon it, &c., it was killed by a great rock dropped on it from the wall.

it sustained without flinching, &c., it bore without trying to run away.

136. **swerved**, drew to the side.

turned tail, ran away.

levelled the iron spikes, bent or broke the projecting bits of iron that were on the frontlet.

137. **despatched the driver**, killed the driver.

he lost his balance, he was overturned.

138. **was dangling in reach, &c.**, hung down so that he could get hold of it.

to swarm up, to climb up by using hands and feet.

to languish, to be carried on with less vigour.

Page

the attention, &c., the efforts of the one side were given mainly to building the mound and of the other to hinder them from doing so.

elevated to a sufficient height, reared so high as to overlook the walls.

inevitable, a thing which must of necessity happen.

139. **reveal a path, &c.**, show a road by which they could make their way into the castle.

forcing an entrance, &c., making by force their way into the castle.

dangerous enterprise, undertaking in which they ran great risk of being killed.

specially selected, &c., chosen because they were more than usually brave and active.

140. **course of procedure**, way of doing the thing.

bee-line, straight line such as a bee was at one time supposed to take instinctively in returning to its hive.

effecting a lodgment, getting in and getting hold of a position they could defend.

141. **involved in their destruction**, caused by their death the death of the whole surprise party.

opportunely thrust out, pushed out at the proper time.

patrol, march carefully round to make sure all was right.

142. **nick of time**, right moment.

it was impossible for it to obtain, &c., it could not in any way get food.

to save his father from, &c., to keep his father from being killed.

143. **to extricate himself, &c.**, to get himself and his men out of a position they could no longer hold.

forlorn hope, the picked men sent forward to open the attack.

obnoxious, dangerous and hateful.

144. **illuminated the scene**, lit up the scene.

in accordance with orders, &c., obeying commands previously given as to what they should do in case of a night attack.

Page

concentrated, drew together in greatest numbers.

145. **cypher**, secret characters, the meaning of which is understood only by those who have the key.

His life or his liberty, &c., he is to be killed or put in prison.

Phalgoon (*Phalgun*), the month corresponding to March.

146. **intrigues**, carefully contrived plots.

extreme caution, very great care.

discovery of his identity, finding out who he really was.

prevent him from saving, hinder him from guarding his father.

147. **to escape notice**, to keep out of sight.

the court was already there, the Rajah, his followers, and attendants were in the palace.

at their evening meal, at supper.

he seemed to be enjoying, &c., seemed to relish or like the food that had been put before him.

superintended the cooking, looked after and given instructions with regard to preparing the food.

148. **carcanet**, a necklace.

something furtive, something that showed she did not wish others to see what she was about, something stealthy.

jewelled chalice, a drinking cup adorned with precious stones.

149. **violating the sanctity**, forcing yourself into a place forbidden, not respecting your father's privacy.

fell unconscious, fainted.

infatuation, irrational devotion.

recognized the loyalty, saw the good faith, the fidelity of.

150. **pay the penalty**, &c., undergo punishment for.

restored to favour, given his old place of honour and trust.

Equally joyous, &c., the faces of the soldiers and the citizens showed that they were quite as happy as Himmut Singh himself was at the way things had turned out.

Page

poured out of the gates, came out of the gates to meet them steadily and continuously, in a stream.

152. **debarred from embellishing**, forbidden by religion from decorating.

chaste and refined, &c., simple and pure, free from extravagance, restrained.

153. **grotesqueness**, extravagance, whimsicality, seemingly purposeless departure from what is usual.

Pantheon, temple of all the gods. The entire body of gods worshipped by the Hindus.

the spectacle presented, &c. Bijapur looked pretty much as it looks now.

defined against, standing out clear on the sky-line.

dominated, looked down on by, thrown into the shade by.

dome of the Gol Gumbaz, the tomb of Ibrahim Adil Shah II, the second largest dome in the world.

154. **St. Mark's**, the cathedral of Venice.

St. Peter's, the great cathedral of Rome, the largest, though not the most beautiful church in the world, covering twice (nearly) the area of St. Paul's, London.

Pantheon, an ancient Roman temple, built in reign of Augustus, the only real building of old Rome still in perfect preservation, now turned into a church, the church of *S. Maria Rotondo*.

combats of animals, fights between wild beasts.

bull-fights, fights on foot and horseback with bulls in circus.

grand tournament, an arrangement whereby knights and soldiers could test against others their skill in arms.

155. **taking part**, having a share, being one of those who fought.

expected to welcome, be glad to purchase the services of.

Suleyman the Magnificent (1520 to 1566). During his reign Turkey reached the highest point of its power and fame.

Page

156. **Knights of St. John.** These knights for at least a couple of centuries prevented the Turks from becoming the dominant power in the Mediterranean.

richly laden argosy, a ship carrying a very valuable freight (lit. ship of Ragusa, an Italian port).

Malabar coast, west coast of India.

Their numbers, &c. The only effect of their being so many was that so many were killed.

157. **killed or driven.** They were killed, or to escape being killed were forced to jump into the sea.

for mercenary motives, for what it would bring him.

158. **Immediate prospect**, a likelihood that war would be soon.

compete in the tournament, be one of those who tried for the prizes offered.

159. **to be thronged**, to be crowded or huddled together.

tier above tier, one row above another.

arena, the space where the struggle took place.

The show opened, the proceedings began with.

160. **more merciful and sportsmanlike**, less cruel and more sporting.

prevalent in southern India, usually followed in southern India.

gored horses, horses torn with the bull's horns.

161. **possibility, &c.**, the likelihood that it would be killed to amuse the Indian holiday makers.

indignation, scornful wrath.

poltroon, cowardly fellow.

162. **playing the inactive rôle**, merely looking on, doing nothing but looking at what others did.

exasperated the elephant, roused the elephant to anger.

in this extremity, in this very dangerous position.

that seemed imminent, it looked as if he would be killed.

163. **a splendid exhibition, &c.**, a fine show of what a rider can do.

Page

the climax, &c., the most highly interesting part of the proceedings.

arduous contest, the fierce and trying struggle.

164. **armour of proof**, armour that had been tested—put to the *proof*—to show that it could not be pierced by spear or cut by sword-stroke.

to do himself justice, to show what he could do, do his best.

crossed by adverse fortune, hindered by bad luck.

tilt at ring, try riding past to carry off hanging ring on point of their lance.

To expedite matters, to hurry on things.

165. **Emperor Akbar.** Akbar (1542 to 1605) was the greatest of the Mogul Emperors.

Jousted at Aspramont, &c. (from Milton's *Paradise Lost*, book i, lines 583-4), fought mock battle.

Aspramont, a castle in Italy, near Nice.

Montalban, a castle in Languedoc, noted in the wars of Charlemagne.

Damasco, Damascus, a very old town in Syria, the scene of several battles during the Crusades.

Trebisond, a town on the Black Sea, of great note and splendour in the Middle Ages.

à outrance, to a decision, to the bitter end.

decide the award, &c., to determine who was victor.

166. **positions in the lists**, places which had been prescribed for them to take before beginning to fight.

vizor, front part of helmet.

167. **good graces**, favourable opinion and good wishes.

chivalrous conqueror, courteous and generous opponent who had beaten him.

final encounter, last of the battles, the battle to settle which of the two was the best knight among the competitors.

had pierced, had gone through.

168. **couched their lances**, put them ready for the fight; directed them straight at each other.

Page

shivered to the hilts, broken to pieces.

could no longer retain, &c., was unable longer to keep his seat in the saddle.

169. **under the humiliation**, under what he thought the disgrace of being beaten.

aimed in quick succession, directed quickly one after another.

Intervened, came between them; separated them.

gross infraction, clear and distinct breaking of well-known rules.

infuriated, in a mad rage.

170. **becoming exhausted**, getting tired out.

temporary madness, insanity for the time being.

redoubled, renewed twice as loudly.

installed as captain, publicly put into the position of head of the body-guard.

171. **recent acquisitions**, gains of territory made a little before.

dissensions, quarrels with one another.

Religious zealots, Mahometans anxious to spread the faith of the prophet.

were inspired, had as their reason for joining in the war.

172. **very conducive**, help greatly.

perilous mission, dangerous task set for him.

fully recovered, completely better.

173. **avenging armies**, armies sent to punish them for their idolatry.

offer was accepted, he was allowed to go to Vijayanagar.

perilous errand, dangerous task or mission.

excite suspicion, make the people wonder why he had come, whether as a friend or as an enemy.

further protection, &c., to make it still less likely that he would be found out.

in emergencies, when sudden and unexpected things happened.

Page

174. **his undertaking**, what he had promised he would do.

specimens of the merchandise, examples of the goods.

infested, crowded into and made themselves troublesome in.

debatable land, parts which belonged now to one kingdom, now to another, and for which there is constant contention.

bidding against each other, one offering a higher reward than the other to those who would enlist.

175. **Tungabhadra**, a tributary of the Kistna.

Cyclopean, a form of building with huge rough blocks, met with in Greece and Italy, and ascribed to the Thracians. It was so called after the Thracian king Cyclops.

defended against, protected from.

176. **spacious quadrangle**, large-sized open space with four sides at right angles to one another. The space occupied by fountains and trees and covered ways.

177. **may inspect**, &c., may closely examine the valuable things he has to show.

178. **Rama**, the hero of the *Ramayana*. According to local tradition, it was near Vijayanagar that Rama first got definite word of his wife Sita, and heard that the forces were gathered together for the attack on Ceylon, and on Ravana, the ten-headed ravisher. The place is held holy, therefore, by the Hindus.

finely-chiselled, clearly cut.

deficient knowledge, his want of words to tell what he knew.

179. **powerfully affect her heart**, rouse up her strongest feelings.

Golden Horn, an inlet from the Bosporous on which Constantinople stands.. It forms the harbour of Constantinople.

a wild longing, &c., a desperate wish to get back to Turkey.

180. **curious intaglio**, a very uncommon jewel with a device sunk into it.

Ayesha was again utilized,

Page

Ayesha was again called on to act as.

181. **unintelligible to all, &c.**, no one but him could understand it.

rest of his merchandise, the other things he had for sale.

assigned to him, given to him to be used.

enhanced by the beauty, he thought more of the message because the messenger was very pretty.

182. **Shiva's fane**, the temple of Shiva, or Siva, the third deity in the Hindu triad—the destroyer.

intervening space of time, the time between the return to his room and midnight.

military preparations, arrangements for defence or for attacking the enemy.

183. **dead silence**, perfect quiet, complete noiselessness.

sough, &c., moaning or whistling noise made by wind.

tremulous foliage, quivering leaves.

vestibule, the entrance hall.

monolithic sculpture, figure carved from a single stone.

184. **more than twenty cubits**, between thirty and forty feet.

canopy, an overhead covering fixed at some height up.

intertwined in labyrinthine mazes, twisted one coil round another so as to form a maze or labyrinth.

tortuous convolutions, turnings and twistings in and out.

unexpectedly stumbled upon, met with by the merest chance.

185. **bael-trees**, quinces.

refrain, part repeated at end of verse, chorus.

audacity in seeking, &c., her boldness in asking a stranger to meet her.

186. **pardon my shamelessness**, forgive my boldness and seeming lack of modesty.

187. **disguise yourself**, dress yourself and take the appearance and character of a page so that no one will know you.

188. **priceless information**, news whose value is of the very highest.

189. **divined the true object**, discovered what the real purpose of Yusuf Khan's visit was.

190. **at a sufficient distance**, far enough back from the river to make it impossible for people on the other side to see it.

in battle array, drawn up in order of battle.

at a moment's notice, as soon as the signal was given.

cross-fire, fire directed from both sides and having the things fired at in the middle.

apparently unconscious, &c., seemingly unaware that they ran any risk.

had decoyed, had led by false pretences into a trap.

191. **doomed advance guard**, the party led across the river by Sidi Hassan and fated to be destroyed.

before it could be reinforced, before help could be brought up to it from the other side of the river.

implored him, begged him earnestly.

important tidings, news that would be of help.

192. **order an immediate, &c.**, bid the soldiers draw back at once.

incite my followers, stir my men to rebellion.

divulge his double-dyed treachery, make known to the soldiers how they had been betrayed by their leader.

193. **appeased them**, brought them to look at matters calmly.

conducted to the presence, brought before.

account for his conduct, explain and justify what he had done.

lowest depths of despair, made to give up all hope.

to leave no stone unturned, to do everything she possibly could to get him freed.

make a long circuit, go a long way round.

Page

194. **to save the vanguard**, to prevent the first division of the advancing army from being wiped out.

from the inmost recesses, hidden in the innermost folds of his turban.

was conferred on, &c. Yusuf Khan was made commander of the advance guard.

195. **to entice the Hindu army**, to lure the Hindus away from their position.

the device succeeded, they got the Indian army to do as they wished.

doubled back, went back the way they had come.

196. **Talikoti.** This great battle was fought somewhere south of Talikota.

Lepanto, a naval battle in which Don John of Austria defeated the Turks, and so prevented them from becoming supreme in the Mediterranean. It was fought in 1571, six years later.

directing the operations, ordering the soldiers what to do.

197. **animated by, &c.** He wished to punish Ram Rajah for having treated himself badly.

in succession, one body after another.

to interpose, to put themselves between.

quailed before, felt cowed and frightened at.

198. **belonging to either side**, some of the elephants belonged to one side and some to another.

did not lose sight, &c., still kept hunting after Ram Rajah.

crowd of fugitives, multitude of people running away.

completed the discomfiture, put the finishing touch to the defeat.

199. **he might have married, &c.**, he would have been thought a good enough match as a husband for one even of the royal family.

200. **realized the seemingly, &c.**, got the things she hoped for though hardly expected to get when a slave to Ram Rajah.

Page

Stamboul, a corruption of three Greek words meaning 'into the city', the name given to the most important part of Constantinople.

201. **successfully defended, &c.**, beaten back the Mahrattas, so that they were unable to plunder or kill us.

Swally (*Suvali*), formerly the seaport of Surat.

terribly distressed, greatly vexed and hurt.

miniature, a painting on a small scale, usually in water colours, on ivory or vellum.

Martyr King, Charles I, who was executed in January, 1649. The Royalists looked on him as a holy martyr.

the great rebellion, the war between king and parliament, 1642-9, in which the 'right divine of kings to govern wrong' was decided to be an unconstitutional maxim in Britain.

202. **ransacked**, searched and all the valuables stolen.

Raighur (*Raigarh*), a hill fort on the Western Ghats, sometimes spoken of as the Gibraltar of India.

Malignant, cavalier, one who fought for King Charles, one of the court party.

Roundheads, nickname given to the supporters of the parliament, or Puritans, in the Civil War.

rebel government, government of parliament and of Cromwell.

Naseby, battle in which King Charles's forces were defeated, 1645.

203. **embroidered stuffs**, cloths or muslin with figures sewn on them in silk or in gold and silver thread, a kind of work for which India was specially famous.

warlike ancestors, forefathers who had been fighters.

prosaic routine, uninspiring round of tasks day after day the same.

repining at, regretting, grumbling greatly at.

from declaring my passion, telling the girl I loved her.

Page

204. **gave me reason to hope,** made me think she might marry me.

analyse the motives, break up into their separate parts the reasons a young man has for doing anything.

advisable, &c., a thing that would have been wise to do.

to inform my uncle, to tell to my uncle what I intended doing.

gray-bearded wisdom, right judgment that comes with age.

Soorti, belonging to Surat.

courage, &c., bravery and trustworthiness.

holsters, leather cases for holding pistols. These were carried in front of the saddle.

205. **mounted and accoutred,** furnished with beasts to ride and arms to defend ourselves.

greeted us, met our eyes.

threw her silver mantle. Milton, the poet here spoken of, wrote:

"Till the moon,
Rising in clouded majesty, at length
Apparent queen, unveiled her peerless light,
And o'er the dark her silver mantle threw."
—*Paradise Lost*, bk. iv, l. 609.

"who ought to be," &c. This was the general opinion of the Royalists at the Restoration. Milton had by his writings, especially his *Defensio Prima, Defensio Secunda*, and *Eikonoklastes*, made himself exceedingly obnoxious to the Royalists. His *Paradise Lost*, the greatest of English epics, from which the quotation is made, was first published in 1667. To the credit of the ruling powers Milton, whom age and blindness made helpless, was not tried as a regicide.

206. **groups of bandits,** bands of robbers.

hovered near us, moved about not far from us, now on one side now on another.

marauders, rogues and thieves out hunting for plunder.

held aloof scowling, kept away from us, looking very angry and very threatening.

Page

an easier prey, someone who could be robbed with less risk.

bivouacked, lay down and slept in the open air.

the poor agriculturists, the poor country people who tilled the land, the peasants and farmers.

chupatties, Indian cakes.

207. **rare luxuries,** things we could seldom indulge in.

for love or money, neither for humanity or kindness nor for any price we could offer.

plain ... tale, a story to tell simply and exactly as it happened.

havildar, a non-commissioned officer of the rank of a sergeant.

208. **a picturesque group,** a body that would have made a very interesting picture.

quilted cotton, cotton on both sides with cotton wool fastened in between.

valour and ferocity, bravery and savagery or cruelty.

A parley ensued, there was a talk between us as to what we each should do.

maharaja (*Shivaji*), the word means the great king.

209. **punctilio,** a formal point of procedure.

surrender our arms, hand over our swords and pistols.

is accessible, can be reached.

bastions, ramparts or fortifications.

killedar (*killádár*), the governor of a fort.

210. **durbar** (also *darbar*), an audience, literally the court of a king or chief. The word is often used as a general name for the local government of a native state.

girt, surrounded or girdled.

no artificial fortifications, no defences save those provided by nature.

extolling, &c., praising highly.

man of blood, man who had put so many to death in wars.

211. **treacherous assassination,** secret murder in which the methods used were even more

Page

opposed to all principles of honesty and fairness.

done to death, caused to be murdered.

face of a devil, a bad, cruel face.

execute his cruel mandates, do the cruel things he bade them do.

scanned his features, examined his face bit by bit carefully.

212. **expressive of kindness**, telling more clearly of a warm heart.

fear and execration, dislike and curses.

Mawali (*Mavalis*, *Mavlas*), Shivaji's best foot soldiers, drawn from the upper valleys of the Ghats.

Hetkuri (*Hetkari*), an inhabitant of the southern Konkan. They were much employed as soldiers by Shivaji.

expressive of mingled, &c., used words that showed they loved him strongly and admired him greatly because he had freed their nation from the foreign yoke of Bijapur.

213. **gadi** (*gaddi*), a cushion to sit on; particularly a king's cushion, a throne.

aigrette, a plume for the head.

doomed to die an evil death. There may be doubts as to whether the death of Sambhaji was evil or not. It was certainly in many ways worthy. Surprised and taken prisoner, he was brought before Aurangzeb, who wished him to become a Mahometan. Sambhaji feeling himself insulted, replied in such a way as to enrage Aurangzeb, who brutally ordered that he should have his tongue cut out, his eyes put out, and then be put to death.

Page

peishwa (*peshwa*), the title of the Prime Minister of the Márátha Kingdom. On the death of Sambhaji the sovereign power passed into the hands of the Peshwa.

214. **immemorial customs**, practices that went as far back as human memory could carry men, that had always been followed.

was suddenly dissipated, brought to an end.

215. **petition for the restoration**, beg for the return.

fairly gravelled, &c., found myself utterly unable to think of an answer.

disinterested benevolence, doing a kindness without expecting any reward.

216. **obstinately opposed**, fought resolutely against.

217. **a wide prospect**, an extensive view.

stalked, stealthily followed.

218. **remarkable agility**, wonderful speed.

numerical superiority, their being greater in number.

219. **opportunely assisted**, helped at the right moment.

Bhowani, so called after the goddess who presented him with it.

221. "**Bhima**" (*Terrible*), the second of the five sons of Panda, and the principal general of the Pandava army. He was taught the use of the club by Dróna.

222. **Dr. Broughton**. About 1651, Gilbert Broughton, an English surgeon, got from Shah Jehan, as a reward for curing his daughter Jahanava, permission for the English to trade in Bengal.